Spanish Today

for
Medical and Emergency Personnel
(School Nurse Edition)

A Medical Spanish Workbook

Written by
Vendla Smith

Zinta Inspired Language
Wichita, KS

D1293620

Copyright © 2020, 2019 by Zinta Inspired Language LLC. All rights reserved.

No part of this work may be reproduced or transmitted in any form by any means, electronic or mechanical, including photocopying and recording, or by any information storage or retrieval system without the prior written permission of Zinta Inspired LanguageLLC unless such copying is expressly permitted by federal copyright law.

All inquiries should be addressed to:
Zinta Inspired Language
2040 S. Rock Road, Suite 90
Wichita, KS 67207

ISBN 9798688476910

Printed in the United States

Disclaimer: These materials are not responsible for any problems or miscommunications between health care and emergency personnel and Spanish-speakers, and assumes no liability herein. The materials should be used as an informational resource and in no way provide medical or treatment recommendations. They should not be used as a replacement for a translator. It is the responsibility of the health care and emergency facility to provide necessary translation services for every encounter.

Contents

Welcome

Welcome to *Spanish Today For Medical and Emergency Personnel!* Here at *Zinta Inspired Language* we have worked hard to develop this manual that will teach you how to better communicate with the Spanish-speaking population and their families.

We live in a world becoming more and more diverse. Many of the people speak different languages, have different backgrounds, and have different cultural aspects about them. In order to better work together we must understand both language and culture.

This program will help you to communicate in the Spanish language, and also give you skills that can teach you how to understand, read, and write better.

This manual is meant to give you the basics of the Spanish language as well as targeted and practical phrases to use in the medical and emergency areas. We sincerely hope that you enjoy your studies in this course!

About This Manual

This course is designed to help you in the areas of speaking, listening, reading, and writing in the Spanish language. The book is divided into the following sections:

- Explanation and Practice:
    - o Includes brief explanations of lessons
    - o Includes practice exercises to do in groups and individually
- Glossary:
    - o Includes all vocabulary words in the book alphabetized in Spanish to English, and English to Spanish
- Answer Key:
    - o Includes all answers to practice exercises.

About the Author

Vendla Smith, M.Ed.
Founder and Director of Zinta Inspired Language

Vendla Smith, founder and director of Zinta Inspired Language, has developed a unique and innovative instructional model that goes beyond 'Words' and 'Mechanics'. This model has proven to remedy both 'visible' and 'invisible' core issues related to communication.

Traditional approaches to language acquisition have always been focused on "studying" it hoping one day to "use" the language conversationally. Vendla's approach to language acquisition enables the learner to actually "use" the language while acquiring it, thereby gaining fluency faster than traditional methods.

Vendla has presented nationally for agencies such as the Department of Defense, Department of Aging, and the National Association for School Nurses Annual Conventions. She has also presented over 150 Industry specific seminars nationwide.

She received her Bachelor of Arts in Foreign Language, State Teaching License, and Master of Education in Curriculum and Instruction. She is currently pursuing her Doctor of Philosophy in Education.

Her vast travel experience and personal interaction with various cultures in many parts of the world has given her a deep understanding of not only languages, cultures, and traditions, but also how to transform the way the learner views and communicates with the world around them.

In 2000 she founded Zinta Inspired Language, a cross-cultural an international language training center. Zinta holds local classes, national industry specific seminars and presentations, and international distance learning from Canada to Ecuador.

What You Will Learn

After completion of this Spanish manual you will be able to perform the basic objectives at a low level. Communication will still be difficult, but you will have some background knowledge that will help you better serve the Spanish-speaking population. Different students will be able to perform at different levels of proficiency based on talent, practice, and previous exposure to Spanish. All students, however, should be able to perform the objectives at a basic level.

STUDY TIPS

First- Give your full attention to the lesson and practice the material over and over. Repetition is a very important part of learning a foreign language.

Second- Speak mentally, aloud, alone, or if possible, with someone else. You must teach your mouth new tricks, so you should first listen then imitate. Practice new words and sentences aloud. Listen to yourself and try to improve.

Third- Read and write vocabulary over and over. Learn to spell the vocabulary words with accent marks.

Fourth- Memorizing new vocabulary takes much practice. Try to spot similarities to Spanish. Be sure you learn the words both from English to Spanish and from Spanish to English. Don't be passive; make up little sentences to yourself using the new words.

Fifth- To expect to know the content of a lesson in English after one time through a drill is the same as expecting to be an expert musician after one practice. Language is a habit.

Sixth – Cognates are word that look alike in Spanish and English such as: elefante, teléfono, televisión, etc. Always look for these because they will help you learn more vocabulary quickly. Concentrate on learning the harder words that don't look like English since the ones that do look like English are so much easier to learn.

Explicación y práctica

Explanation and Practice

"The simple explanations and practice exercises in this section of the Spanish Today manual help to enhance learning and recollection of the language in an easy to use manner."

La pronunciación
Pronunciation

Introducción

Spanish pronunciation is phonetic thanks to their vowels. Vowels in Spanish are pronounced shorter than in the English language. For example, when we pronounce the letter "A" in English, we might say "aaaaahhh". In Spanish, it is shorter, we would say "ah" which may sound clipped. Each of the vowels are pronounced very short.

Los sonidos vocales – A, E, I, O, U

The vowel sounds are the most important sound to learn when pronouncing Spanish words. Each vowel only has one sound.

A = (ah)   as in father or law
E = (eh)   as in egg or let
I = (ee)   as in meet or leaf
O = (oh)   as in over or go
U = (oo)   as in zoo or do

¡Práctica!

A. Las Sílabas: Practice pronouncing the following syllables.

1. na ra sa pa da
2. ne re se pe de
3. ni ri si pi di
4. no ro so po do
5. nu ru su pu du

6. du po si re na
7. na re si po du
8. di sa ne pu ro
9. ri ne pa so du
10. pe ra di no su

Los sonidos consonantes

Most of the Spanish letters are pronounced the same as in English. The consonants that are pronounced differently than English are as follows:

> h- is always silent. (hola)
> j- is the happy letter. Whether it laughs ha, or he, j always sounds like an "h"   (José, jalapeño)
> ll-when the two letters come together they sound like "y" (llama)
> ñ- this nosey letter talks through her nose. She sounds like the "ny" in canyon. Maybe you have heard of "el niño"?
> q- is always followed by "u". Qu sounds like a very hard "k". (queso)
> rr- is always rolled. Try this: Erre con erre carro.
> z- she looks like a backwards "s" and has the same sound. (zapato)
> c- sounds like the "c" in coat except when followed by an e or i. It sounds like the "s" in soon then. (casa, cebra)
> g- sounds like go except before e or i, then it is like the "h" in home. (gato, gente)

La pronunciación de palabras

In order to correctly pronounce any word in Spanish you must first divide the word into syllables and pronounce every letter in each of the syllables. There is no silent "E" at the end of words, so you pronounce that letter as well. Spanish is so phonetic that if you can say the word, you can probably spell it!

Note: If there is a written accent on a vowel, then you put the stress on that letter.
> Example: teléfono, lápiz, estómago

¡Práctica!

B. Las Palabras: Practice pronouncing the following words. Concentrate on the vowel sounds.

mano	brazo	pierna	pelo	cara
uña	dedo	estómago	cerebro	muñeca
ojo	muela	garganta	cabeza	espalda
nariz	diente	labio	pie	cuello
oreja	oído	boca	lengua	corazón

C. Las Frases: Practice pronouncing the following Spanish sentences. Be sure to pronounce the questions as if you were asking a question instead of reading a statement.

1. ¿Cómo se llama usted?
2. Yo me llamo Julio.
3. ¿Tiene usted fiebre?
4. Sí, yo tengo fiebre y me siento enfermo.
5. ¿Cuántos años tiene usted?
6. Yo tengo cuarenta y cinco años.

D. A Escuchar: Listen as your instructor pronounces some words. Fill the blanks with the correct vowel sound. A – E – I – O – U

1. V___c___

2. C__br___

3. B__ls___

4. L__br___

5. ___rc___ ___r___s

Formal e informal

Formal and Informal

Introducción

Respect is so important with the Spanish language, that there are two ways of saying everything. There is a formal and an informal way.

The formal "you" in Spanish is "usted". The informal "you" in Spanish is "tú".
Example: ¿Cómo está **usted**?   ¿Cómo estás **tú**?

The formal would be used with someone who you could speak with in a professional manner, someone who you do not know well, or someone older. The informal would be used when speaking with a child or someone you are very close to.

If you are not a native speaker, you may not be criticized for using the wrong form, but you may be politely corrected.

¡Práctica!

A. *Identificación:* Identify if you would use the formal "you" (usted), or the informal "you" (tú) with the following people.

1. someone you just met
2. a child
3. your teacher
4. your grandmother
5. your best friend
6. your pet
7. a customer
8. your boss
9. someone you know well
10. someone obviously younger than you

Communication is MORE than just words! Let's learn some interpersonal communication skills by learning about the wall that divides us!

THE WALL THAT DIVIDES US

Did you know that there is an invisible wall between you and another person you meet when you don't know each other well?

There is a wall that we can't see. It is completely invisible to our eyes, but it is made up of many different bricks. The bricks are formed from all that we have learned throughout our lifetime and the experiences that we have had both good and bad.

The wall does not allow us to really "see" who that other person is. We "think" we know who they are and what they are like, but the wall is very deceptive and made up of different assumptions. This wall can prevent us from getting to know the person for who they really are.

The bricks may be made of the following:

- Stereotypes
- Negative Facial Expression
- Negative Body Language
- Misunderstandings
- Avoidance
- Lack of Politeness
- Negative Tone of Voice
- Lack of Respect
- Expressive vs. Non-Expressive
- And many more!

To truly communicate with someone, we must break down these walls. Communication is done through more than just words. We can send both positive and negative messages apart from our words. We also communicate with our body language, facial expression, gestures, and tone of voice. We must make sure that we are not saying something positive while at the same time communicating something negative through our actions. The following skills can help tear down the walls and build up trust in the first 5 minutes of meeting someone:

1. When greeting someone, be sure to show a level of respect they expect. Use Mr., Mrs., Miss, sir, or ma'am when necessary. The Hispanic culture is more formal, so they are accustomed to hearing titles and words of courtesy such as: Nice to meet you, please, and thank you.

2. Be sure to give your undivided attention to who you are talking to. Do not look down at your phone, computer, etc. Look at the person in the face because the Hispanic community is very relational and that is what is expected. It is confusing when someone is looking away, to know who they are speaking to.

3. Be sure to greet everyone including the children. It only takes a moment to acknowledge everyone so be sure to do that and not ignore anyone. A simple "Buenos días" is sufficient while making eye contact with everyone.

When we are open, warm, and friendly, barriers come down. Many difficult situations can be defused when our words match our body language, facial expression, and tone of voice. When our words do not match the interpersonal communication, mistrust can be built instead of trust, so be careful what you communicate beyond words!

¡Práctica!

A. La Cultura: Think about how you would answer the following questions.

1. What are some of the invisible bricks that separate us when meeting someone for the first time?

2. Beyond words, what are some ways in which we communicate with another person?

3. What are some ways that positive messages can be sent?

4. What are some ways that negative messages can be sent?

5. Why is it important to make sure that our interpersonal communication matches our verbal communication?

Saludos y presentaciones
Greetings and Introductions

Introducción

Because first impressions are very important, you will want to know your common greetings well. Even though you may not speak much Spanish, knowing the greetings can start your conversation out right and make it a little smoother.

Saludos populares

Buenos días. = Good morning.
Buenas tardes. = Good afternoon.
Buenas noches. = Good evening/night.
Hola. = Hello. (informal)

Using a title of respect always helps to begin the conversation well. You may want to add in the following titles of respect after each greeting. Example: Buenos días, señora.

señor - Mr., sir
señora - Mrs., ma'am
señorita - Miss

¡Práctica!

A. Saludos: Which greeting would you use at the following times?

1. 8:00 a.m.
2. 7:00 p.m.
3. 11:00 p.m.
4. 4:00 p.m.
5. 6:00 a.m.

¿Cómo está?

¿Cómo está? = How are you? (formal)
¿Cómo estás? = How are you? (informal)
Muy bien. = Very well.
Bien. = Fine.
Así-así. = So so.
Mal. = Bad.
Muy mal = Very bad.

¡Práctica!

B. Cortesía: Ask the following people how they are doing and tell how they would respond.

1.   2.   3.

4.   5.

¿Cómo se llama?

¿Cómo se llama? = What is your name? (formal)
¿Cómo te llamas? = What is your name? (informal)
Me llamo _____. = My name is _____.
Mucho gusto. = Pleased to meet you.

¡Práctica!

C. Situaciones: Ask the following people what their name is, tell how they would respond, and tell them that you are pleased to meet them.

1. Octavio Paz
2. Gloria Estefan
3. Horacio Quiroga
4. Diego Rivera
5. Pablo Picasso

Despedidas populares

Adiós. = Good-bye
Hasta luego. = See you later.
Hasta pronto. = See you soon.

Did you know...

The Hispanic culture is a very polite culture. Please and thank you are always used. When meeting someone for the first time, one must always tell them that they are pleased to meet them. When entering a room, one should greet everyone in the room.

¡Práctica!

D. Conversación: Practice greeting friends in Spanish, asking their names, asking how they are doing, and giving a farewell.

E. Diálogo: Practice reading the following dialogues aloud in Spanish. After reading each dialogue, translate the dialogue from Spanish to English.

Diálogo 1:
The nurse is meeting the adult patient for the first time.

Enfermera: Buenas tardes. Me llamo Marisa. ¿Cómo se llama usted?
Paciente: Me llamo Humberto Castillo.
Enfermera: Mucho gusto Señor Castillo. ¿Cómo está usted?
Paciente: Así-así.
Enfermera: Espere un momento, por favor. (Wait a moment, please.)

Diálogo 2:
The teacher is meeting a student for the first time.

Maestra: Buenos días. ¿Cómo se llama?
Estudiante: Me llamo Juan.
Maestra: Me llamo Irene. Mucho gusto Juan.
Maestra: ¿Cómo está usted?
Estudiante: Muy mal. Tengo una nota mala. (I have a bad grade.)
Maestra: Un momento, por favor.

F. Diálogo: Complete the following dialogue.

Recepcionista: _____ días. _____ Alicia.
            ¿Cómo _____?
Cliente: _____ Jorge Rodriguez.
Recepcionista: Mucho _____. ¿Cómo
_____?
Cliente: No _____ bien. Muy _____.
Recepcionista: Espere un momento, por favor.

G. Traducción: Translate the following conversation from Spanish to English.

Doctor: Buenos días.

Paciente: Hola.

Doctor: ¿Cómo está usted?

Paciente: Bien, gracias. ¿Y usted?

Doctor: Muy bien. ¿Cómo se llama usted?

H. Reacciones: How would you respond to the following?

1. Hola.
2. ¿Cómo se llama usted?
3. Buenas tardes.
4. Hasta luego.
5. Bien, gracias. ¿Y usted?
6. Buenos días.
7. Me llamo _____.
8. Chao.
9. ¿Cómo está usted?
10. Hola.

I. ¿Cómo está?: How would the following people answer how they are doing?

¿Cómo está usted?

1.   2.   3.   4.   5.

A conversar
¿Cómo se llama?

Conversación #1:

You are meeting a patient for the first time. Greet them, ask them how they are doing, ask them their name, and give a farewell.

Conversación #2:

You are in the cafeteria and a Spanish speaking person just set next to you. Greet them, ask them how they are doing, tell them how you are doing, ask them their names, tell them your names, and give a farewell.

A escribir
¿Cómo está?

Write out a greeting and introduction dialogue between a patient and caregiver using the vocabulary that you have learned. Be sure to add a greeting, have each ask how the other is doing, and ask and give names.

El alfabeto

The Alphabet

Introducción

The alphabet in Spanish is called the "abecedario". The Spanish alphabet consists of 30 letters including ch, ll, ñ, and rr. You might see the "ch" separated into "c" and "h" on some occasions.

These letters are considered single letters and are alphabetized as such in the Spanish dictionary. So if you were looking for a word that begins with "ch", you would have to look past the "c" section completely. The "w" is for words of foreign origin so there is typically not a section for "w" words in the Spanish dictionary.

Letter	Pronunciation Key
A	ah
B	be
C	ce
CH	che
D	de
E	eh
F	efe
G	ge
H	hache
I	ee
J	jota
K	ka
L	ele
LL	eh-yea
M	eme
N	ene
Ñ	en-yea
O	oh
P	pe
Q	coo
R	ere
RR	erre
S	ese
T	te
U	oo
V	be
W	doble ve / doble oo
X	equis
Y	ee-griega
Z	zeta

¡Práctica!

A. ¿Cómo se escribe?: Practice spelling the following names aloud using Spanish letters.

1. María Sánchez
2. Octavio León
3. Roberto García
4. Enrique Rodríguez
5. Alejandra Avila
6. Manuel Mendoza
7. Rosa Zapata
8. Alfonso Fernández
9. Mónica Medrano
10. Gabriela Monroy

B. ¿Cómo se escribe su nombre?: Practice asking and answering the following question. Be sure to spell out your name.

¿Cómo se llama usted? --   What is your name?

Me llamo _____. --   My name is _____.

¿Cómo se escribe su nombre? -- How do you spell (write)
                                              your name?

**Note: *The majority of the time you will use the alphabet will be to spell your name. Be sure to practice this enough to be able to do it smoothly and slowly.*

Expresiones de cortesía
Courtesy Expressions

Introducción

The best way to get started speaking a language is to know some useful phrases to help you communicate. The following expressions are very important to know before trying to communicate in Spanish.

Do you speak English?	¿Habla inglés?
Do you speak Spanish?	¿Habla español?
Yes/No.	Sí/No.
I speak a little.	Hablo un poco/poquito.
Please speak slower.	Por favor, hable más despacio.
Repeat please.	Repita, por favor.
Do you understand?	¿Entiende?
I don't understand.	No entiendo.
I understand.	Entiendo.
How can I help you?	¿En qué puedo ayudarle?
Excuse me.	Con permiso.
I'm sorry!	¡Lo siento!
How do you say....?	¿Cómo se dice....?
Thank you.	Gracias.
You're welcome.	De nada.

¡Práctica!

A. Traducción: Match the Spanish phrases with the English translations.

_____1. Gracias.

a. I speak a little.

_____2. No entiendo.

b. You're welcome.

_____3. ¿En qué puedo ayudarle?

c. Speak slower.

_____4. Hable más despacio.

d. I understand.

_____5. ¿Habla español?

e. I don't understand.

_____6. Hablo español.

f. Repeat please.

_____7. Hablo un poquito.

g. I speak Spanish.

_____8. ¿Entiende?

h. Thank you.

_____9. Entiendo.

i. Do you speak Spanish?

_____10. Repite, por favor.

j. Do you understand?

_____11. De nada.

k. How can I help you?

_____12. Lo siento.

l. Excuse me.

_____13. Con permiso.

m. I'm sorry.

B. ¿Cómo se dice?: How would you say the following phrases in Spanish?

1. How do you say....?

2. I'm sorry.

3. Yes.

4. Repeat, please.

5. Thank you.

6. Do you understand?

7. You're welcome.

8. Do you speak English?

9. I don't understand.

10. Excuse me.

You do NOT have to speak in complete sentences to communicate!
Let's learn how to communicate a LOT with just a few "key" words!

PACK YOUR BAGS

Did you know that you can throw out about 80% of what's being said and still understand someone? You really only have to catch a couple of key words in a sentence to understand what the person is trying to say. If you can throw out 80% of what THEY say, you can also throw out 80% of what you THINK you have to say to communicate.

If you feel overwhelmed with remembering all the complete sentences and are wondering how you will actually learn to USE the language, then this next part is for you!

When beginning a language, many students can't remember the beautiful questions and statements such as "¿Cuál es su número de teléfono?" However, we don't need to remember all those words in order to ask someone for their phone number. What is the key word or words in the question? Answer: teléfono.

Now let's take these skills and pack an imaginary backpack in our minds to take with us out in the "real world" when we don't have our book or notes.

You already have many word and phrases in your backpack. Try to answer the following questions without using your notes. Remember you don't have to answer using an entire sentence!

- What is a greeting in Spanish?
- How do you ask for a name?
- How do you ask someone how they are doing?
- How do you answer how you are doing?
- How do you ask for a phone number?
- How do you ask for an address?

You may have answered:

Buenos dias,
¿Cómo se llama?
¿Cómo esta?
Bien
Teléfono
Dirección

If you could pull out a key word or two, you gained a LOT of information using only a few words. You were able to greet someone, ask them their name, how they are doing, their phone number, and their address. As you move through learning a new language, look for "key words" that you can easily pack up in your imaginary backpack in your mind to use when you need them.

Many words are the same or similar as English such as: hospital, rodeo, hotel, elefante, teléfono, computadora, diccionario, etc. When you run across these words, take note of them and pack them in your minds as well. This can help build your vocabulary very quickly in the language.

¡Práctica!

A. Palabras Importantes: Think about how you would answer the following questions?

1. Do you have to understand every word someone says in order to understand them?

2. How do you communicate with someone if you can't remember the entire sentence?

3. What are some ways that you can pack the imaginary backpack in your mind?

Los números
Numbers

Introducción

We use numbers on a daily basis. Some ways that we use numbers to talk about dates, tell time, age, number of family members, phone numbers, addresses, cost and money, etc.

Numbers are extremely important to know and be able to use. The most important numbers to learn are 0-10 because many numbers can be expressed digit by digit.

Las reglas

A. Informational numbers are stated as one digit at a time. Some informational numbers include addresses, telephone, and social security numbers.

For example: 678 Sunset Blvd. would be written as:
  seis, siete, ocho Sunset Blvd.

B. Years must be stated as whole numbers.

For example: 1977   would be written as:
  mil novecientos setenta y siete

C. You use *cien* for exactly one hundred and *ciento* for any number over one hundred.

D. Beginning with the number thirty-one, Spanish numbers must be written in three separate words. "y" means "and"

 For example: 31   would be written as:
    treinta y uno

E. *Mil* does not have a plural form, but *millón* does.

For example: un millón, dos millones, tres millones, etc.

Los números 0-10

0   cero
1   uno
2   dos
3   tres
4   cuatro
5   cinco
6   seis
7   siete
8   ocho
9   nueve
10 diez

¿Cuál es el número de teléfono.... de su casa?
de su trabajo?
celular?

What is the phone number…of your house?
of your work?
cellular?

¿Cuál es su dirección?

What is your address?

Los números

0	cero	60	sesenta
1	uno	61	sesenta y uno
2	dos	62	sesenta y dos....etc.
3	tres		
4	cuatro	70	setenta
5	cinco	71	setenta y uno
6	seis	72	setenta y dos...etc.
7	siete		
8	ocho	80	ochenta
9	nueve	81	ochenta y uno
10	diez	82	ochenta y dos....etc.
11	once	90	noventa
12	doce	91	noventa y uno
13	trece	92	noventa y dos....etc.
14	catorce		
15	quince		
16	dieciséis	100	cien
17	diecisiete	101	ciento uno
18	dieciocho	102	ciento dos....etc.
19	diecinueve		
		200	doscientos
20	veinte	300	trescientos
21	veintiuno	400	cuatrocientos
22	veintidós...etc.	500	quinientos
		600	seiscientos
30	treinta	700	setecientos
31	treinta y uno	800	ochocientos
32	treinta y dos...etc.	900	novecientos
40	cuarenta	1,000 mil	
41	cuarenta y uno	2,000 dos mil.....etc.	
42	cuarenta y dos...etc.		
		1,000,000 un millón	
50	cincuenta	2,000,000 dos millones	
51	cincuenta y uno		
52	cincuenta y dos...etc.		

¡Práctica! - *Números 0-10*

A. Número de teléfono: Read the following telephone numbers asking the following question before each number.

¿Cuál es su número de teléfono?
1. 573-3927
2. 453-9704
3. 129-6754
4. 836-0584
5. 269-3566
6. 802-8495

B. Escribir: Write the numerals for the following telephone numbers.

1. tres – nueve – dos – siete – cero – uno - nueve

2. cuatro – ocho – cinco – uno – siete – seis - cero

3. cinco – nueve – tres – uno – ocho – seis – cero

4. siete – dos – cuatro – cinco – seis – cuatro - tres

5. uno – nueve – ocho – cero – cinco – siete - dos

6. cuatro – seis – tres – ocho – cero – nueve - cinco

¡Práctica! - *Números 0-20*

C. Asociaciones: Match the numbers in written form to the correct digits on the right.

1. _____ diecinueve
2. _____ cinco
3. _____ once
4. _____ catorce
5. _____ seis
6. _____ trece
7. _____ ocho
8. _____ dieciocho
9. _____ tres
10. _____ veinte
11. _____ uno
12. _____ nueve
13. _____ quince
14. _____ cuatro
15. _____ diez
16. _____ dieciséis
17. _____ dos
18. _____ diecisiete
19. _____ doce
20. _____ siete

a. 10
b. 17
c. 12
d. 2
e. 9
f. 19
g. 6
h. 13
i. 4
j. 11
k. 7
l. 16
m. 3
n. 18
o. 15
p. 8
q. 20
r. 14
s. 5
t. 1

¡Práctica! - Numbers 11-100

D. Asociaciones: Match the numbers in written form to the correct digits on the right.

1. _____ treinta y cinco

2. _____ cincuenta

3. _____ ochenta y tres

4. _____ veinte

5. _____ diez

6. _____ trece

7. _____ cuarenta y ocho

8. _____ dieciocho

9. _____ setenta y siete

10. _____ veintidós

11. _____ sesenta y uno

12. _____ noventa y nueve

13. _____ cien

14. _____ cuarenta y dos

15. _____ diecinueve

16. _____ dieciséis

17. _____ veintiséis

18. _____ diecisiete

19. _____ doce

20. _____ cincuenta y cinco

a. 19

b. 17

c. 12

d. 26

e. 99

f. 35

g. 10

h. 13

i. 42

j. 83

k. 55

l. 16

m. 77

n. 18

o. 100

p. 48

q. 22

r. 20

s. 50

t. 61

E. La clase: Practice reading the following numbers.

1. 42 estudiantes
2. 28 papeles
3. 91 sillas
4. 37 mesas
5. 74 casas
6. 59 plumas
7. 83 libros
8. 65 diccionarios

¡Práctica! - *Numbers 100-1,000,000*

F. Traducción: Practice translating the following numbers from Spanish to English.

1. doscientos cincuenta y tres

2. ochocientos setenta y uno

3. mil quinientos veintiséis

4. cuatro mil setecientos ochenta y nueve

5. tres millones cuatrocientos treinta y cuatro mil novecientos cuarenta y dos

G. Números: Practice translating the following numbers from English to Spanish.

1. 743

2. 251

3. 1,398

4. 5,836

5. 2,937,417

H. Matemáticas: Write out the following equations and solve.

(y = and   son = are)
Modelo: 100 + 100 =
          cien y cien son doscientos

1. 150 + 200 =

2. 210 + 130 =

3. 400 + 240 =

4. 500 + 500 =

5. 700 + 100 =

6. 1,500 + 5,500 =

Did you know...

The word "educación" refers more to the person's upbringing or manners than formal education. "Mal educado" means "rude" whereas "bien educado" means well-mannered. Formal education is often referred to as "enseñanza".

El género
Gender

Introducción

Before you begin to speak Spanish, there is a little basic Spanish grammar that you need to know.

A noun is a word used for a person, place, thing, or idea. All nouns in Spanish are considered either masculine or feminine. Feminine nouns usually end in -a or -as. And masculine nouns usually end in -o or -os. Nouns that refer to women are usually feminine, and nouns that refer to men are usually masculine.

    Examples: braz<u>o</u> (masculine) = arm
               cas<u>a</u> (feminine) = house
               chic<u>as</u> (feminine) = girls
               chic<u>os</u> (masculine) = boys

Nouns that do not end in -o or -a must be found in a dictionary to determine its gender. Most Spanish nouns are masculine.

¡Práctica!

A. Identificaciones: Are the following nouns masculine or feminine?

1. cabeza
2. piernas
3. brazo
4. pelo
5. dedos
6. pie
7. cara
8. hombros

Los artículos
The Articles

Introducción (Los Artículos Definidos)

There are four ways to say the word "the" in Spanish. The word "the" will change depending if the word is masculine, feminine, singular, and plural.

Take a look at the chart below:

THE		
	Masculine	Feminine
Singular	el	la
Plural	los	las

Example:
      el lib<u>ro</u> – (the book) this word is masculine and singular
      los lib<u>ros</u> – (the books) this word is masculine and plural
      la mes<u>a</u> – (the table) this word is feminine and singular
      las mes<u>as</u> – (the tables) this word is feminine and plural

¡Práctica!

A. ¿Qué es?: How would you say "the" for the following nouns?

Example: zapato = el zapato
             comida = la comida
             carro = los carros
             iglesia = las iglesias

1. blusa
2. latas
3. libro
4. dinero
5. muchacho
6. papel
7. computadoras
8. ropa

B. La Clase: Fill in the blanks with el, la, los, or las.

1. _____*la*_____ tarea (example)

2. _____ preguntas

3. _____ profesora

4. _____ diccionarios

5. _____ libro

6. _____ secretaria

7. _____ cuadernos

8. _____ casas

9. _____ papeles (m)

10. _____ reglas

11. _____ marcador (m)

12. _____ exámenes (m)

13. _____ estudiantes (m)

14. _____ maestra (f)

15. _____ plumas

16. _____ oficina

Introducción (Los artículos indefinidos)

There are four ways to say the words "a, an, and some" in Spanish. These words will change depending if they are masculine, feminine, singular, and plural.

Take a look at the chart below:

A, An, Some		
	Masculine	Feminine
A, An (Singular)	un	una
Some (Plural)	unos	unas

Example:
    un lib<u>o</u> – (a book) this word is masculine and singular
    unos lib<u>ros</u> – (some books) this word is masculine and plural
    una mes<u>a</u> – (a table) this word is feminine and singular
    unas mes<u>as</u> – (some tables) this word is feminine and plural

¡Práctica!

C. Los Artículos: Give the proper translation for the following objects.

Some vocabulary words you will need are:

libro-book, mesa-table, clase (f)-class, carro-car, ventana-window

1. the book

2. the books

3. a book

4. some books

5. the table

6. the tables

7. a table

8. some tables

9. the class

10. the classes

11. a class

12. some classes

13. the car

14. the cars

15. a car

16. some cars

17. the window

18. the windows

19. a window

20. some windows

Did you know...

The term "familia" usually means extended family which might consist of members such as father, mother, children, spouses of children, grandparents, aunts, uncles, and cousins. Family ties are usually very strong and often live together in one household.

D. Identificación: Write the correct indefinite (un, una, unos, unas) or definite (el, la, los, las) articles in the spaces below.

Hint:
(the) - el, la, los, las
(a, an, some) - un, una, unos, unas

1. _____ (the) carro

2. _____ (a) carro

3. _____ (the) carros

4. _____ (some) carros

5. _____ (the) pluma

6. _____ (a) pluma

7. _____ (the) plumas

8. _____ (some) plumas

9. _____ (the) libro

10. _____ (a) libro

11. _____ (the) libros

12. _____ (some) libros

13. _____ (the) mesa

14. _____ (a) mesa

15. _____ (the) mesas

16. _____ (some) mesas

La familia
The Family

Introducción

Many Hispanic families still live in extended families. They may live with grandparents, aunts, uncles, or cousins. However, these extended families are giving way to more of a nuclear family especially in the cities.

Most Hispanic people have two last names. The first one is from their father, and the last one is the mother's maiden name. The father's last name is the one that is usually used when addressing someone. When a woman marries, she usually keeps her maiden name but on very formal occasions will add her husband's name to the end of hers.

Los miembros de la familia tradicionales

el abuelo-grandfather
la abuela-grandmother
los abuelos-grandparents

el hijo-son
la hija-daughter
los hijos-children

el tío-uncle
la tía-aunt
los tíos-aunts and
uncles

el padre-father
la madre-mother
los padres-parents

el nieto-grandson
la nieta-granddaughter
los nietos-grandchildren

el sobrino-nephew
la sobrina-niece
los sobrinos-nieces and
nephews

el hermano-brother
la hermana-sister
los hermanos-brothers
and sisters

el esposo-husband
la esposa-wife
los esposos-spouses

el primo-cousin (male)
la prima-cousin (female)
los primos-cousins

el novio-boyfriend/ fiancé
la novia-girlfriend/ fiancé

Los miembros de la familia no tradicionales

Because there are more and more non-traditional families today, I have included some extra vocabulary that may help in dealing with these non-traditional families.

la madrastra- step mother
el padrastro- step father
la hermanastra- step sister
el hermanastro- step brother
la hijastra- step daughter
el hijastro- step son
la cuñada- sister in law
el cuñado- brother in law
la suegra- mother in law
el suegro- father in law

¡Práctica!

A. *Mi familia:* Complete each phrase with the appropriate vocabulary word.

1. El hermano de mi madre es mi _____.
2. La hija de mi padre es mi _____.
3. El hijo de mi tía es mi _____.
4. Los hijos de mi esposo son mis _____.
5. Mi hermana es la _____ de mi madre.
6. El padre de mi madre es mi _____.

Did you know...

Traditionally, the Hispanics have two last names. Many do not have a middle name. For example, in the name "Miguel Lopez García", "Miguel" is the first name, "Lopez" is the last name (father's family name), and "García" is the second last name (mother's maiden name). If only one name is needed, they usually choose the father's family name.

El árbol genealógico de Ana

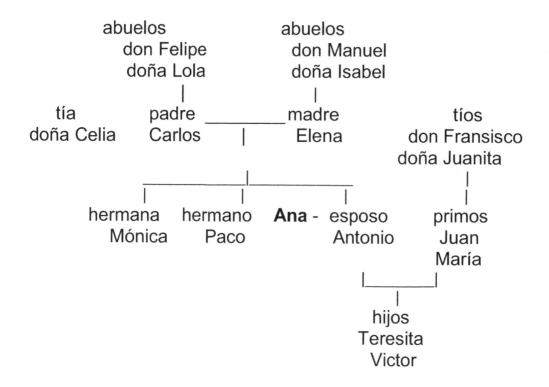

B. La familia de Ana: Are the following statements about Ana's family true *(cierto)* or false *(falso)*?

1. Felipe es el padre de Carlos.
2. Mónica es el hermano de Ana.
3. Celia es la madre de Ana.
4. Juanita es la esposa de Fransisco.
5. Elena es la abuela de Paco.
6. Víctor es el hijo de Antonio.
7. Juan y María son hermanos.
8. Manuel e Isabel son hermanos.
9. Carlos es el esposo de Elena.
10. Carlos es el hijo de Manuel e Isabel.

C. ¿Cómo se llama?: Answer the following questions according to Ana's family.

1. ¿Cómo se llama la madre de Ana?

2. ¿Cómo se llama el hermano de Teresita?

3. ¿Cómo se llaman los abuelos de Mónica?

4. ¿Cómo se llaman los padres de Juan y María?

5. ¿Cómo se llama la tía de Paco?

D. ¿Quién es?: Describe the relationships of the members of the Solano family below to the others.

Modelo: Eduardo: Alicia/Roberto y Estela
Eduardo es el esposo de Alicia y el padre de Roberto y Estela.

1. Roberto: Eduardo y Alicia/ Gloria
2. Estela: Eduardo y Alicia/ Raúl
3. Ana: Jorge y David/ Estela y Paul
4. Patricia: Jorge, Ana y David/ Roberto y Gloria
5. David: Eduardo y Alicia/ Jorge y Ana

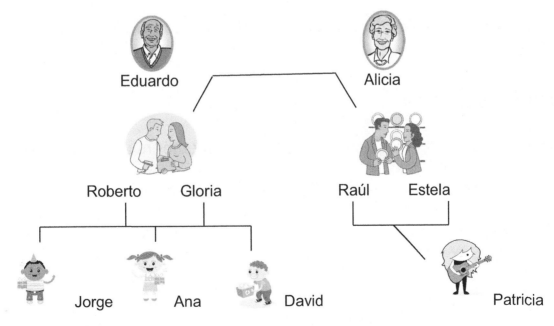

47

Preguntas sobre la familia

Question: What are the differences between the following phrases?

¿Cómo se llama usted?
¿Cómo se llama él?
¿Cómo se llama ella?

Answer: ¿Cómo se llama usted? means "What is *your* name?"
¿Cómo se llama él? means "What is *his* name?"
¿Cómo se llama ella? means "What is *her* name?"

These phrases literally mean What do you call yourself?
What does he call himself?
What does she call herself?

Note: When translating Spanish to English, we translate ideas rather than just words.

Estado civil

Many words that refer to a woman end in "a" and to a man end in "o".

casado/a = married
soltero/a= single
divorciado/a= divorced
viudo/a= widower/widow

Example: A married woman would be "casada" whereas a single man would be "soltero".

¡Práctica!

E. Estado civil: Tell whether the following members of Ana's family are married or single.
Example: Don Felipe - Don Felipe es casado.

1. Ana
2. Celia
3. Juan
4. Elena
5. Manuel

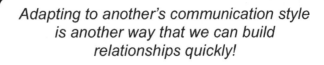

Adapting to another's communication style is another way that we can build relationships quickly!

HIGH VS LOW EMOTIVE PERSONALITIES

Did you know that there are different communication "styles"? Some people use a visual aspect, and some are more words-oriented when it comes to communication. Understanding the difference will help us more effectively communicate with the other person.

There are high and low emotive personalities. Everyone falls on the scale at different places, but the higher emotive person can communicate very differently from the low emotive person. This can lead to misunderstandings and a feeling of not being heard. If handled appropriately, even stressful situations can be de-escalated quickly.

The following describes the characteristics of each of the types. You may find that you fall strictly to one or the other, or you may fall somewhere in the middle. Knowing your communication style and understanding and identifying someone else's communication style is key to building trust with them.

High Emotive:

A High Emotive person typically expressing themselves through the following ways:

- Reads body language very well, they communicate with their body language and facial expressions
- Are not direct and go roundabout in their speaking
- Focused on non-verbal communication rather than verbal
- Mistrust is built when your words don't match your body language.

Low Emotive:

A Low Emotive person typically expresses themselves through the following ways:

- Are more direct
- They communicate with their words more than with their body language
- Focused on verbal rather than non-verbal communication.

It's important to be aware of where we fit and can see where the other person fits. When we communicate we want to be able to match the other person in order to help tear down the wall. If they are high emotive, you might have to come up a little to match them by communicating with body language and your facial expressions and focusing less on the words. If someone is low emotive, you may have to meet them at their level in order to communicate and ask them to explain to you the situation so that they can ue their words.

Can you see how much more we would get along if everyone were able to adapt to fit the communication styles of the person with whom they are speaking?

¡Práctica!

A. La comunicación: Think about how you would answer the following questions.

1. Why are communication styles important?

2. What are some characteristics of a high emotive person?

3. What are some characteristics of a low emotive person?

4. What communication style are you?

5. What are some specific ways you would communicate with an upset high emotive person?

6. What are some specific ways you would communicate with an upset low emotive person?

Los días, los meses y las fechas
Days, Months, and Dates

Introducción

It is difficult to get along well if you can't express days, months or dates. When talking about days, months, and dates, it is easier to first know some basic vocabulary that deal with the elements of time.

Day	día
Month	mes
Year	año
Week	semana
Hour	hora
Minute	minuto
Today	hoy
Tomorrow	mañana
Yesterday	ayer
Next month	próximo mes
Next week	próxima semana
Next year	próximo año

¡Práctica!

A. Vocabulario: Fill in each of the blanks with the appropriate Spanish word.

1. There are fifty-two _____ in a year.

2. There are seven _____ in a week.

3. There are twelve _____ in a year.

4. Ayer was _____ (day of the week).

5. Mañana es _____ (day of the week).

6. Hoy es _____ (day of the week).

Introducción de los días

The week begins on Monday in many Spanish-speaking countries. Please note that on the calendar Monday is to the left, and Sunday is to the right. Note that days of the week and months of the year are generally not capitalized in Spanish.

Days of the Week

MAYO

LUNES	MARTES	MIERCOLES	JUEVES	VIERNES	SABADO	DOMINGO
	1	2	3	4	5	6
7	8	9	10	11	12	13
14	15	16	17	18	19	20
21	22	23	24	25	26	27
28	29	30	31			

Months of the Year

enero- January
febrero- February
marzo- March
abril- April
mayo- May
junio- June
julio- July
agosto- August
septiembre- September
octubre- October
noviembre- November
diciembre- December

¡Práctica!

B. Los días: Give the day before and the day after each of the following.

ayer= yesterday   hoy= today   mañana= tomorrow

<u>ayer</u>   <u>hoy</u>   <u>mañana</u>

1. _____ jueves   _____

2. _____ lunes   _____

3. _____ sábado   _____

4. _____ miércoles   _____

5. _____ domingo   _____

6. _____ martes   _____

7. _____ viernes   _____

C. Los meses: Fill in the following blanks with Spanish vocabulary words.

1. Thanksgiving always falls on a _____.

2. Christmas is celebrated in the month of _____.

3. Today is _____.

4. What month has 28 days?

5. What three months are considered summer?

6. What month and day is Mother's Day celebrated?

7. What day does the Spanish calendar begin with?

D. Los días: Find and circle the days of the week in the puzzle from the list on the left. Then translate the words on the left to your native language.

Search for:

lunes

martes

miércoles

jueves

viernes

sábado

domingo

A	W	R	N	W	A	Y	R	Q	U	S	T	W	E	A
T	S	D	M	E	O	Y	G	P	S	V	M	P	R	D
T	H	O	R	S	D	A	Y	A	A	L	R	C	M	A
R	F	M	B	A	L	D	D	D	M	Y	K	U	I	Y
R	R	I	G	T	X	S	A	B	A	D	O	X	E	F
E	I	N	F	U	M	E	Y	O	R	E	J	B	R	D
Q	D	G	J	R	R	N	S	S	T	V	U	W	C	M
U	A	O	V	D	Y	D	P	N	E	E	M	R	O	O
A	Y	D	V	I	E	R	N	E	S	S	N	H	L	N
L	D	A	Y	Y	M	J	A	C	E	M	R	G	E	J
S	S	U	N	D	L	U	N	E	S	B	D	F	S	F
S	E	I	L	P	R	E	V	N	C	B	L	H	Y	D
A	W	D	R	G	Y	V	I	L	N	V	X	C	R	W
N	M	K	G	K	P	E	C	M	O	N	D	A	Y	A
T	U	E	S	G	F	S	F	R	I	C	J	G	A	Y

Calendario azteca

54

E. Los meses: List the following months according to their season.

el invierno (winter)   la primavera (spring)

el verano (summer)   el otoño (fall)

F. Días y meses: Answer the following questions about days and months.

1. What is the first day of the week on the American calendar?

2. What is the first day of the week on the Spanish calendar?

3. What months of the year are the following holidays?

    Navidad (Christmas)

    Día de los padres

    Día de gracias

    Día de San Valentín

    Cinco de Mayo

4. What is the day in the middle of the week called?

5. What month does school usually start?

6. What day do we vote?

Introducción de la fecha

The most common way of expressing dates in Spanish is to remember the popular holiday "Cinco de Mayo". This date shows the pattern for describing all dates in Spanish.

5 de mayo de 2014 (May 5, 2014)
19 de enero de 1971 (January 19, 1971)

Remember: The months in Spanish are not capitalized.

If you are wanting to talk about the first day of the month in Spanish you must use the word "el primero" *the first*. For all other dates, you just use the number in Spanish.

1 de marzo - el primero de marzo
2 de marzo - dos de marzo
3 de marzo - tres de marzo, etc.

Years in Spanish are pronounced as regular numbers are. The year 1971 would be read as number one thousand nine hundred seventy one "mil novecientos setenta y uno". The English custom of saying the year 1971 as "nineteen seventy one" is not followed. The year 2002 would be read as "dos mil dos".

¡Práctica!

G. La fecha: How would you express the following dates in Spanish?

1. July 26, 2013

2. August 8, 1989

3. March 4, 1997

4. January 14, 2002

5. May 27, 1999

H. Días festivos: What are the dates for the following U.S. holidays?

1. Valentine's Day _____

2. Christmas Day _____

3. New Year's Day _____

4. Independence Day _____

5. Halloween _____

Las citas

In order to schedule an appointment, you would need to add "Su cita es el..." and then the date, which means "Your appointment is the ...".

Example: October 8, 2014

"Su cita es el <u>ocho de octubre</u> de <u>dos mil catorce</u>."
              (date)   (year)

I. Las citas: Practice scheduling appointments for the following dates.

1. April 10, 2015

2. June 16, 2014

3. September 9, 2015

4. November 21, 2014

¿Qué hora es?

What Time Is It?

Introducción

Telling time in Spanish is not difficult. The word "time" in Spanish is rarely used when expressing the time. In Spanish, it is customary to use the word "hora" *hour* when expressing time. You can literally ask, "What is the hour?" and answer "The hour is....".

Describing the current time.

¿Qué hora es?	=	What time is it?
¿Qué horas son?	=	What time is it?

There are two ways of asking someone the time in Spanish. You may choose the one you prefer.

You must have two words at the beginning of each phrase when you tell someone the time.

Es la = It's   (This phrase is singular, therefore use only with one
o'clock.)
Son las = It's (This phrase is plural, therefore use between the
hours of two and twelve.)

Es la una. = It's one o'clock..
Son las dos. = It's two o'clock.
Son las tres. = It's three o'clock.
Son las cuatro. = It's four o'clock.
   etc.

When describing a quarter after, just add "y cuarto".

Es la una y cuarto. = It's a quarter past one.
Son las dos y cuarto. = It's a quarter past two.
Son las cinco y cuarto. = It's a quarter past five.

When describing half past, just add "y media".

Es la una y media. = It's one thirty.
Son las siete y media. = It's seven thirty.
Son las diez y media. = It's ten thirty.

For all the other times, you just add the minutes after the hour using the word "y".

Es la una y diez. = It's ten after one.
Son las ocho y cuarenta. = It's eight forty.
Son las once y cincuenta. = It's eleven fifty.
Son las nueve y treinta y cinco. = It's nine thirty-five.

Es mediodía. = It's noon.
Es medianoche. = It's midnight.

Describing future time.

When describing future time, just substitute "a" for "es" and "son".

¿A qué hora.....? = At what time.....?

A la una. = At one o'clock.
A las dos. = At two o'clock.
A las cuatro y media. = At four thirty.
A las once y cuarto. = At eleven fifteen.

A mediodía. = At noon.
A medianoche. = At midnight.

A.M. and P.M.

de la mañana = a.m., in the morning
de la tarde = p.m., in the afternoon
de la noche = p.m., in the evening/night

Son las dos y media de la tarde. =   It's two thirty p.m.
A las ocho y cuarto de la mañana. = At eight fifteen a.m.

¡Práctica!

A. ¿Qué hora es?: Ask the question "What time is it?" in Spanish before answering using the following times.

1. 3:00 p.m.
2. 5:50 p.m.
3. 7:15 a.m.
4. 8:00 a.m.
5. 6:30 p.m.
6. 10:10 a.m.
7. 4:15 p.m.
8. 12:00noon
9. 7:45 p.m.
10. 12:00midnight

B. ¿Qué hora es?: Give the times on the clocks.

_____

_____

_____

_____

C. ¿A qué hora comes?: Tell what time you eat.

1. 11:05 p.m.

2. 1:20 a.m.

3. 9:35 a.m.

4. 6:40 p.m.

5. 2:00 a.m.

6. 12:00midnight

D. ¿A qué hora...? Write the answers in Spanish according to the following answers in English below. Use the Present tense. *Watch out for the subject changing in every sentence.*

Ejemplo :

¿A qué hora comes anoche (last night)? (11:05 p.m.)
– Yo como a las once y cinco de la noche.

1. ¿A qué hora lees el periódico cada mañana? (5:25 a.m.)

2. ¿A qué hora abre la escuela cada día? (7:35 a.m.)

3. ¿A qué hora estudias el domingo? (6:40 p.m.)

4. ¿A qué hora regresa del cine tu hija? (midnight)

5. ¿A qué hora miras la telenovela cada semana? (1:20 p.m.)

6. ¿A qué hora bebe la leche caliente el niño? (10:30 p.m.)

7. ¿A qué hora comes en el trabajo todos los días? (noon)

8. ¿A qué hora llegan a la escuela los estudiantes cada día? (8:45

    a.m.)

La escuela

The School

Introducción de los empleados de la escuela

The School Nurse often times refers to other positions in the school while speaking with parents. The following is a list of common school staff.

administrator	el administrador/ la administradora
para	el/la asistente
principal	el director/ la directora
bus driver	el conductor/ la conductora
coach	el entrenador/ la entrenadora
counselor	el consejero/ la consejera
custodian	el guardián/ el guardiana
teacher	el maestro/ la maestra
librarian	el bibliotecario/ la bibliotecaria
nurse	el enfermero/ la enfermera
psychologist	el psicólogo/ la psicóloga
receptionist	el/ la recepcionista
security guard	el/ la guardia de seguridad
therapist	el/la terapista

¡Práctica!

A. ¿Quién es?: Tell what school staff member is described below.

1. This person takes care of all of the books in the school.

2. This person tests students.

3. This person keeps the school clean.

4. This person takes many calls and makes appointments.

5. This person keeps everyone safe in the school.

6. This person deals with many scrapes and bruises.

7. This person is the head of the school.

8. This person is responsible for getting the kids to school and home again.

9. This person is the head of the classroom.

10. This person helps the teacher.

11. This person is in charge of a sport.

12. This person helps children with specific problems.

Introducción de los cuartos de la escuela

The School Nurse often times refers to other rooms in the school while speaking with parents. The following is a list of common school rooms.

auditorium	el auditorio
bathroom	el baño
cafeteria	la cafetería
class	la clase
computer lab	el laboratorio de computadoras
counseling office	la oficina del consejero/a
gymnasium	el gimnasio
library	la biblioteca
nurse's office	la oficina del enfermero/a
teacher's lounge	el cuarto de maestras

¡Práctica!

B. ¿Qué cuarto?: Match the English word with the correct translation.

_____1. auditorium   a. el baño

_____2. bathroom   b. la biblioteca

_____3. cafeteria   c. el gimnasio

_____4. class   d. el laboratorio de computadoras

_____5. computer lab   e. el cuarto de maestras

_____6. counseling office   f. la oficina del enfermero/a

_____7. gymnasium   g. la clase

_____8. library   h. el auditorio

_____9. nurse's office   i. la oficina del consejero/a

_____10. teacher's lounge   j. la cafetería

Introducción de las materias escolares

The following is a list of common school subjects in elementary through college.

algebra	el álgebra
art	el arte
biology	la biología
chemistry	la química
drama	el drama
English	el inglés
geography	la geografía
history	la historia
literature	la literatura
math	las matemáticas
music	la música
physical education	la educación física
psychology	la psicología
reading	la lectura
science	la ciencia
social studies	los estudios sociales
sociology	la sociología
Spanish	el español
theater	el teatro
writing	la escritura

¡Práctica!

C. Identificación: Tell what school subject that each picture represents.

1.

2.

3.

4.

5.

6.

7.

8.

9.

10.

11.

12.

D. A Leer: Look over the following advertisement and answer the questions on the next page.

COLEGIO
SAN MARCO

- Cursos Básicos

    matemáticas, español, ciencias, historia, francés, inglés

- Cursos Especializados y Tecnológicos

    electrónica, fotografía, mecánica, carpintería, artes plásticas, computación

- Clases Preparatorias para la Universidad

    literatura, cálculo, biología, astronomía, química, geografía, bellas artes, sociología, psicología, filosofía

Horario de Clases:

lunes   8:00 a 5:00
martes   8:00 a 5:00
miércoles 8:00 a 3:00
jueves   8:00 a 5:00
viernes   8:00 a 3:00
sábado   8:00-12:00
domingo cerrado

Para información:

Profe. D. García, Director
Viveros de Coyoacan, 29C
tel. 6-59-32-39

La Comprensión – Colegio San Marco

1. Under what course category is math?
2. Under what course category is carpentry?
3. How many days of the week is the school open?
4. What specialized courses does the school offer? (list in English)
5. What college prep courses does the school offer? (list in English)
6. Who do I contact if I want more information?

A conversar
¿Qué clase tiene usted?

Vocabulario útil:
    Tengo… – I have
    ¿Tienes…? – Do you have?
    ¿Cuál es tu clase favorita?

Conversación #1:

You are a student at a high school and are seeing a good friend on the first day of school. Greet each other and ask the courtesy questions then ask what classes you have.

Conversación #2:

You are a new student at a college and are trying to meet a friend. Greet the friend, ask them what classes they have, exchange phone numbers, and ask them for their favorite class.

Introducción de las materiales de la escuela

The following is a list of items found in an office or school setting.

backpack	la mochila
bag	la bolsa
book	el libro
calculator	la calculadora
chalkboard	la pizarra
computer	la computadora
desk	el escritorio
dictionary	el diccionario
eraser	la goma/ el borrador
flag	la bandera
folder	la carpeta
marker	el marcador
notebook	el cuaderno
paper	el papel
paperclip	el clip para papel
pencil	el lápiz
pen	la pluma/ el bolígrafo/ el lapicero
ruler	la regla
schedule	el horario
scissors	las tijeras
stapler	la engrapadora
student desk	el pupitre
trash	la basura

¡Práctica!

E. Busqueda: Find and circle the office and school supplies. Then, translate the words on the left.

Search for:

regla

libro

pluma

lápiz

papel

cuaderno

mochila

examen

diccionario

bandera

```
B  W  R  L  I  B  R  O  C  E  R  T  W  E  N
E  S  B  A  C  A  T  S  A  N  E  Y  G  R  A
I  K  O  P  S  N  A  Y  S  A  G  R  C  M  T
S  A  M  I  A  D  K  E  T  B  L  L  L  I  A
B  M  I  Z  T  E  S  X  U  A  A  O  X  E  O
O  U  N  S  W  R  M  A  I  N  G  J  C  R  I
L  L  G  E  M  A  A  M  I  A  V  U  U  C  R
U  P  O  B  E  Y  D  E  N  E  E  M  A  O  A
A  Y  D  A  J  V  O  N  L  E  Y  B  D  L  N
S  L  E  P  A  P  J  A  C  E  M  R  E  E  O
I  S  U  L  N  L  U  N  E  S  B  D  R  S  I
N  V  O  M  O  C  H  I  L  A  B  L  N  Y  C
N  W  D  R  T  Y  V  I  L  N  V  X  O  R  C
E  M  K  G  A  P  E  C  M  O  N  D  I  Y  I
T  U  E  S  P  F  S  F  R  G  N  I  X  O  D
```

Materiales de la oficina

71

F. Identifica: Circle the name of the picture of each item listed.

1.   libro   bandera   mochila

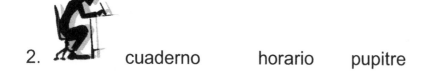

2.   cuaderno   horario   pupitre

3.   bolígrafo   regla   goma

4.   pizarra   tijeras   lápiz

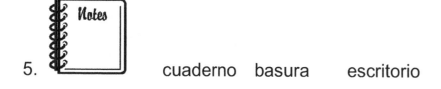

5.   cuaderno   basura   escritorio

6.   pluma   papel   lápiz

G. En la escuela: Below, several *cosas* (things) that you would find in the *escuela* (school) are described. Write the Spanish word for the item being described. More than one answer may be possible. The first one has been done for you.

Vocabulario útil:el papel, el estudiante, el lápiz, el cuaderno, el maestro, la silla, la pizarra, el escritorio, el diccionario, la pluma

1. This is a writing utensil that has an eraser.   *el lápiz*

2. This is the person who teaches you.

3. This is another writing utensil that often does not have an eraser.

4. This is what you use to look up words you don't know.

5. This is the person in the classroom that learns.

6. This is what you keep your papers in so that they are organized.

7. This is what you write on.

8. This is what a teacher generally grades papers on.

9. This is what the teacher writes on at the front of the class.

10. This is what the students sit on during class.

Palabras interrogativas

Interrogative Words

Introducción

Question words are important when you do not know a language well. They are very useful to communicate an entire idea with one word, as well as help you understand someone's question easier.

 Quién – Who?

 Cuál – Which?

 Cuánto – How much? How many?

 Cómo –How?/ What?

 Qué – What?

 Cuándo – When?

 Por qué – Why?

 Dónde – Where?

Más información

- When referring to more than one person, **quién** takes the plural form **quiénes**

¿Quiénes son los criminales?   Who are the criminals?

- When referring to more than one item, **cuál** takes the plural form **cuáles**

¿Cuáles programas miras en la televisión?   What (which) TV shows do you watch?

- When referring to more than one item, **cuánto** takes the plural form **cuántos / cuántas**

¿Cuántos libros tienes?   How many books do you have?

¿Cuántas horas en un día?   How many hours are in a day?

¡Práctica!

A. Traducción: Give the translation for each of the following words from English to Spanish.

1. Why?
2. Where?
3. How?
4. What?
5. When?
6. Who?
7. Which?
8. How many?

B. *Situación:* What question word would you need to use in each of the following situations?

1. You did not hear what the other person said.

2. The co-worker wants to know the reason for the meeting.

3. You do not know a person in the room.

4. The vendor has two shirts and wants to know which one you want.

5. The teacher needs to know the number of students in the class.

6. You want to know how the office got so messy.

7. You want to know where the child hurt himself/herself.

8. You want to know the time of the party.

9. You want to know the price of the souvenir.

10. Your friend wants to know where you are going.

11. The teacher wants to know the reason the child did not get the homework done.

12. You have to use the restroom but don't know where it is located.

13. Your husband needs to know when you will be ready to go.

Did you know...

"Fiesta" means party, but it is more than just a get-together. It is an elaborate celebration. "Fiesta nacional" is the term used for an official holiday. Many of the local dates for holidays change from country to country such as Mother's Day and Father's Day and can catch a foreigner by surprise.

Preguntas para registración

Enrollment Questions

Introducción de preguntas básicas

Common basic informational questions used in the medical and emergency fields are below. You do not need to answer in a complete sentence. Most of the time, complete sentences are not used.

1. ¿Cómo se llama (usted)?
   Me llamo…

2. ¿Cómo está (usted)?
   Bien, gracias.

3. ¿Dónde vive (usted)?
   Yo vivo en…..

4. ¿De dónde es (usted)?
   Yo soy de….

5. ¿Cuál es su número de teléfono?
   Mi número de teléfono es…

6. ¿Cuál es su dirección?
   Mi dirección es…

¡Práctica!

A. Cierto/Falso: Are the following answers appropriate responses to the questions?

1. ¿De dónde es usted? Yo vivo en Los Angeles.
2. ¿Cómo está? Me llamo María.
3. ¿Cuál es su número de teléfono? 358
4. ¿Cómo se llama? Muy bien, gracias.
5. ¿Dónde vive (usted)? Yo soy de Argentina.
6. ¿Cuál es su dirección? 328-928-2938

Introducción de preguntas de más información

Obtaining basic information from patients and their families is not difficult, and the choices for answers are limited. The following questions can help you get the personal information needed to fill out paperwork.

What is your name?	¿Cómo se llama usted?
What is the child's name?	¿Cómo se llama el niño/la niña?
What is your full name?	¿Cuál es su nombre completo?
What is the child's full name? niño/a?	¿Cuál es el nombre complete del
What is your address?	¿Cuál es su dirección?
What is your home phone number?	¿Cuál es el numero de teléfono de su casa?
What is your age?	¿Cuál es su edad?
What is the child's age?	¿Cuál es la edad del niño/a?
What is your date of birth?	¿Cuál es la fecha de su nacimiento?
What is his/her date of birth?	¿Cuál es la fecha de su nacimiento?
When was he/she born?	¿Cuándo nació él/ella?
Single, married, or divorced?	¿Soltero, casado, o divorciado?
What is the name of the nearest relative or friend?	¿Cuál es el nombre de familia o amigo/a más cercano?
What is the phone number of the nearest relative or friend?	¿Cuál es el numero de teléfono de su familia o amigo/a más cercano?
What is your occupation?	¿Cuál es su ocupación?
What is the name of the company where you work?	¿Cómo se llama la compañía donde trabaja?
Does he/she have insurance?	¿Tiene él/ella seguros (aseguranza)?
What is your insurance company?	¿Cuál es su compañía de seguros?

What is your policy and group number?	¿Cuál es su número de póliza y grupo?
What is your zip code?	¿Cuál es su código postal?
What is your work telephone number?	¿Cuál es su numero de teléfono de trabajo?
Can I see your identification?	¿Puedo ver su identificación?
Does your child have siblings?	¿Su niño/a tiene hermanos?
How many?	¿Cuántos?
How many people live in your house?	¿Cuántas personas viven en su casa?
Do both parents live with the child?	¿Ambos padres viven con el niño/a?
Who is responsible for the child?	¿Quié es responsible por el niño/a?
What languages are spoken at home? casa?	¿Cuáles lenguas están hablado en
In case of an emergency, whom should we call?	¿En caso de emergencia, a quién debemos llamar?
How does your child get to school?	¿Cómo llega su niño/a a la escuela?
Who brings/picks up your child?	¿Quién trae/recoge a su niño/a?

¡Practica!

A. Preguntas: Fill out the following information about yourself in Spanish. Try to do it without looking back at the questions. You do not have to answer honestly, but your answers should make sense. After answering all questions, look back on the previous page to make sure that you understood all the questions.

1. ¿Cómo se llama usted?

2. ¿Cuál es su dirección?

3. ¿Cuál es el número de teléfono de su casa?

4. ¿Cuál es la edad del niño/a?

5. ¿Cuál es la fecha de su nacimiento?

6. ¿Dónde nació usted?

7. ¿Su niño/a tiene hermanos?

8. ¿Cuál es el nombre de su familia o amigo/a más cercano?

9. ¿Cuál es el número de teléfono de su familia o amigo/a más cercano?

10. ¿Cuántas personas viven en su casa?

11. ¿Cuáles lenguas están hablado en casa?

12. ¿Quién trae/recoge a su niño/a?

13. ¿Tiene él/ella seguros (aseguranza)?

Los partes del cuerpo

Parts of the Body

Introducción

After learning the parts of the body, it is easy to learn to express pain. The following pages contain both exterior and interior body parts. The interior body parts are similar to the scientific names inEnglish.

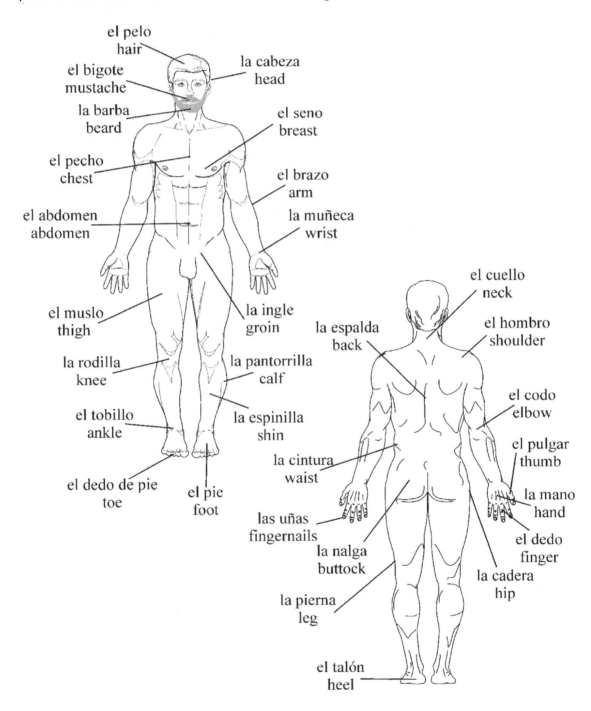

el pelo
hair

el bigote
mustache

la barba
beard

el pecho
chest

el abdomen
abdomen

la cabeza
head

el seno
breast

el brazo
arm

la muñeca
wrist

el muslo
thigh

la rodilla
knee

el tobillo
ankle

el dedo de pie
toe

la ingle
groin

la pantorrilla
calf

la espinilla
shin

el pie
foot

el cuello
neck

la espalda
back

el hombro
shoulder

el codo
elbow

el pulgar
thumb

la mano
hand

el dedo
finger

la cadera
hip

la cintura
waist

las uñas
fingernails

la nalga
buttock

la pierna
leg

el talón
heel

¡Practica!

A: *Los partes del cuerpo:* Point to the following body parts as you say the name of them in Spanish.

1.dedo	2. naríz	3. pierna	4. brazo
5.pie	6. ojo	7. pelo	8. hombros
9.cabeza	10. uñas	11. codo	12. rodilla
13.muñeca	14. cadera	15. boca	16. oreja
17.lengua	18. cintura	19. dedos de pie	20. espalda

B: *¿Qué parte?:* Name the part of the body that is described below.

1. This part is located at the top of the body.

2. These parts help us stand up.

3. Women often paint these parts.

4. These are often stubbed.

5. A belt goes around this part.

6. A purse is often held by these.

7. A seat belt often goes around these parts.

8. This part allows us to move our head around.

9. The part we often sit on.

10. This part often aches when we lift very heavy objects.

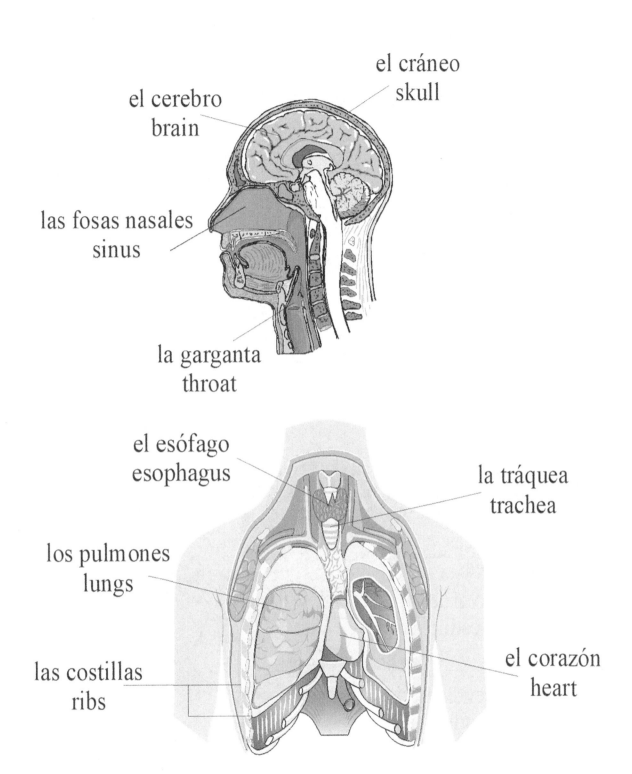

el cerebro
brain

el cráneo
skull

las fosas nasales
sinus

la garganta
throat

el esófago
esophagus

la tráquea
trachea

los pulmones
lungs

las costillas
ribs

el corazón
heart

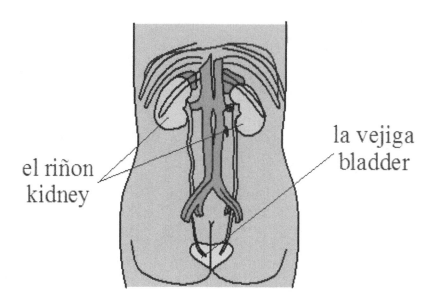

el riñon
kidney

la vejiga
bladder

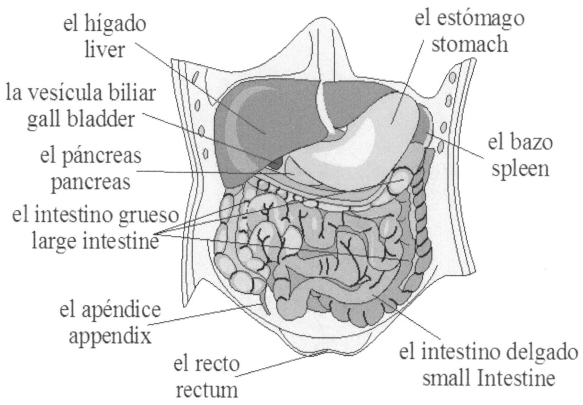

el hígado
liver

la vesícula biliar
gall bladder

el páncreas
pancreas

el intestino grueso
large intestine

el apéndice
appendix

el recto
rectum

el estómago
stomach

el bazo
spleen

el intestino delgado
small Intestine

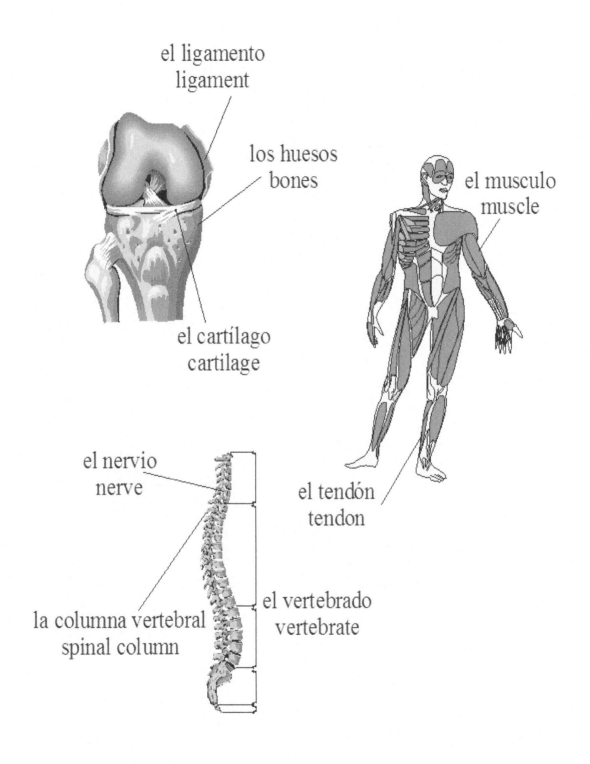

el ligamento
ligament

los huesos
bones

el cartílago
cartilage

el musculo
muscle

el nervio
nerve

el tendón
tendon

la columna vertebral
spinal column

el vertebrado
vertebrate

85

el corazón
heart

la arteria
artery

el ventrículo
ventricle

la vena
vein

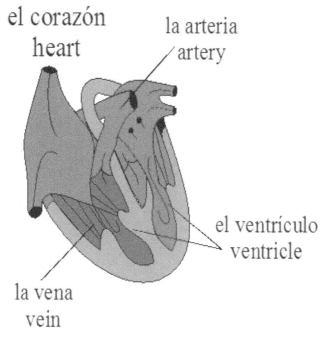

el lente
lens

la córnea
cornea

la pupila
pupil

la piel
skin

el poro
pore

el folículo
follicle

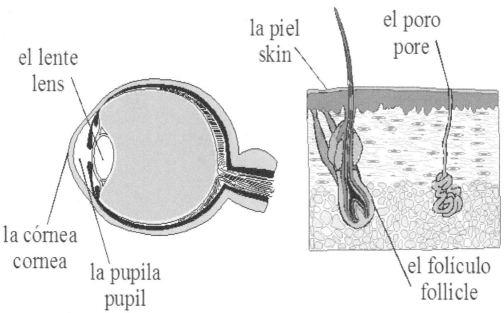

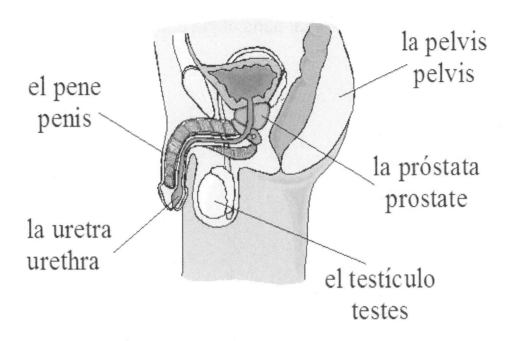

el pene
penis

la pelvis
pelvis

la próstata
prostate

la uretra
urethra

el testículo
testes

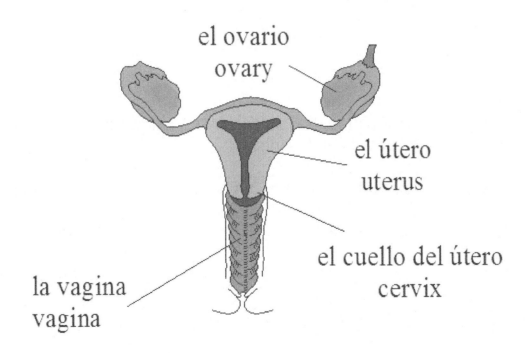

el ovario
ovary

el útero
uterus

el cuello del útero
cervix

la vagina
vagina

¡Practice!

C: Partes interiores: Tell what parts of the body would be affected by the following:

1. strep throat

2. sprained wrist

3. broken leg

4. cold with congestion

5. broken neck

6. heavy drinking

7. diabetes

8. heart attack

9. head injury

10. nausea

D: ¿Dónde está?: Point to the location of the following body parts as you say the name of them in Spanish.

1. corazón	2. pulmones	3. riñones	4. estómago
5. intestinos	6. apendice	7. cerebro	8. garganta
9. bazo	10. esófago	11. vesícula biliar	12. hueso
13. vejiga	14. columna vertebral		

Parts of the Face

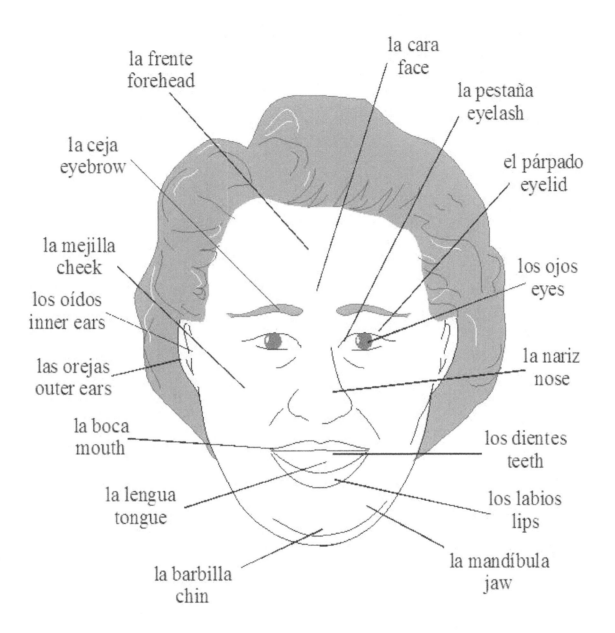

la frente
forehead

la cara
face

la pestaña
eyelash

la ceja
eyebrow

el párpado
eyelid

la mejilla
cheek

los ojos
eyes

los oídos
inner ears

las orejas
outer ears

la nariz
nose

la boca
mouth

los dientes
teeth

la lengua
tongue

los labios
lips

la barbilla
chin

la mandíbula
jaw

¡Practica!

E: *Los partes de la cara:* Point to each of the parts of the face and say them in Spanish. Can you do it without looking in your book?

F: *¿Dónde le duele?:* Write a complete sentence telling what hurts on each of these patients.

1.

2.

3.

4.

G: *¡Me duele!:* Write a sentence telling that each of these body parts hurt.

1. stomach

2. foot

3. hand

4. teeth

5. head

6. arm

7. leg

8. throat

Los dolores

Aches and Pains

Introducción

Talking about aches and pains is fairly easy in Spanish if you know your body parts.

If you want to ask someone if they hurt, you say:

¿Le duele?

If you want to ask someone if they hurt in a specific part of the body you simply add the body part after "le duele".

¿Le duele la cabeza? = Does your head hurt?
¿Le duele el estómago? = Does your stomach hurt?

They will answer the question with the phrase "Me duele".

Me duele. = I hurt.
　　　Or
Me duele la cabeza.
Me duele el estómago.

¡Practica!

A: La traducción: Translate the following dialogue between "el doctor" and "el paciente".

D:　Me llamo Dr. Jones.　¿Le duele?

P:　Sí, me duele mucho.

D:　¿Le duele el brazo?

P:　No, no me duele el brazo.

D:　¿Le duele la garganta?

P:　No, no me duele la garganta.

D:　¿Le duele la cabeza?

P:　No, no me duele la cabeza.

D:　¿Dónde le duele?

P:　Me duele el dedo de pie.

Introducción de más dolores

If you want to ask someone if they hurt in a specific part of the body you ask:
¿Tiene usted dolor de (part of the body)?

Example: ¿Tiene usted dolor de cabeza?
　　　　　Do you have a headache?
They would answer:
Sí, tengo dolor de cabeza.　Or　No, no tengo dolor de cabeza.
Yes, I have a headache.　　　Or　No, I don't have a headache.

¡Practica!

B: Más dolores: Read the following questions and statements substituting the given vocabulary words under the questions for the italicized word.

1. ¿Tiene usted dolor de estómago?　No, no tengo dolor de *estómago.*

   garganta/　espalda/　cabeza/　ojos/　hombros

2. ¿Tiene usted dolor de pie?　No, no tengo dolor de *pie.*

   pierna/　pecho/　brazo/　dedo de pie/　cuello

Introducción de hablar de otra persona

You have learned that when talking about *your* (2nd person) aches and pains, you use "le duele". You have also learned that when talking about *my* (1st person) aches and pains, you use "me duele". When talking about *his or her* (3rd person) aches and pains you also use "le duele".

¡Practica!

C: Los dolores: Make Spanish sentences using the following.

Ejemplo: Juan/ espalda

Juan le duele la espalda. (Juan's back hurts.)

1. María/ nariz
2. Fernando/ mano
3. yo (I)/ lengua
4. Jorge/ oído
5. usted (you)/ pulgar

D: Identificación: Identify the following body parts in Spanish.

1.

2.

3.

4.

5.

E: *¿Dónde te duele?:* Ask what hurts in the following pictures then answer.

1.

2.

3.

Introducción de escala de dolor

There are many cultural problems with the pain scale. When a person is not accustomed to "rating" things, it is very difficult to understand. It can be best illustrated with a 3x5 index card as shown below.

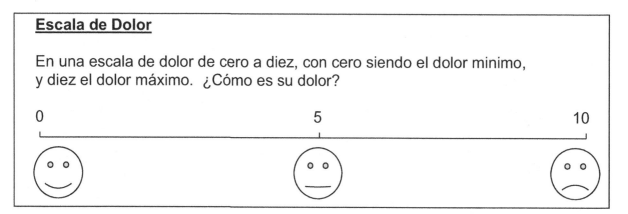

Pain Scale
On a pain scale from 0 to 10, with 0 being the least pain and 10 being the maximum pain. What is your pain like?

Las citas

Appointments

Introducción

You do not need to understand every word in order to understand what someone is asking. If you can catch the "key" words, this will help you to understand what they are trying to ask. As you look at the statements below, concentrate on being able to communicate the "key" words instead of memorizing all of the questions and phrases.

Ejemplo:

You could learn: *Va a tener que esperar un momento.*
Or you could simply say: *Un momento.*

I would like to see the doctor.	Quisiera ver al doctor.
Do you have an appointment today?	¿Tiene usted una cita hoy?
I have an appointment with the doctor at nine o'clock.	Tengo una cita con el doctor a las nueve.
With which doctor?	¿Cuál es su doctor?
Did you bring your insurance card?	¿Trae su seguro médico?
What is your policy number and group number?	¿Cuál es su número de póliza y grupo?
Have a seat please.	Siéntese, por favor.
Follow me please.	Sígueme, por favor.
You are going to have to wait a moment.	Va a tener que esperar un momento.
The doctor still hasn't arrived.	El doctor todavía no ha llegado.
The doctor is going to be late.	El doctor va a llegar tarde.

The doctor will see you in a minute.	El doctor lo verá en un minuto.
Your appointment has been canceled.	Su cita se ha cancelado.
Do you want to make another appointment?	¿Quiere usted hacer otra cita?
Fill out this form, please.	Llene esta forma, por favor.
Sign here.	Firme aquí.
Where is the bathroom?	¿Dónde está el baño?
Where is the pharmacy?	¿Dónde está la farmacia?
Where is the laboratory?	¿Dónde está el laboratorio?
You can pick up your medicine at the pharmacy.	Pase a recoger sus medicinas a la farmacia.
I prefer to change my appointment.	Prefiero cambiar mi cita.
What is your......?	¿Cuál es su.....?
...first name?	...primer nombre?
...last name?	...apellido?
...complete name?	...nombre completo?
...nationality?	...nacionalidad?

¡Practica!

A: ¿Cierto o falso?: Read each question and statement. If the response is appropriate and makes sense, write "cierto" (true). If the response is not appropriate and does not make sense, write "falso" (false).

1. ¿Tiene usted una cita hoy?
   Sí, tengo una cita con el doctor a las diez y media.

2. ¿Cuál es su doctor?
   El doctor va a llegar tarde.

3. ¿Dónde está el baño?
   Firme aquí.

4. ¿Dónde está la farmacia?
   Sígueme, por favor.

5. ¿Trae su seguro médico?
   Su cita se ha cancelada.

6. ¿Quiere usted hacer otra cita?
   Prefiero cambiar mi cita.

B: Una traducción: Translate the following dialogue from Spanish to English.

Recepcionista: Buenas tardes.
Paciente: Buenas tardes. Quisiera ver al doctor.
Recepcionista   ¿Tiene usted una cita hoy?
Paciente: Sí, tengo una cita a las once y cuarto.
Recepcionista: Bien. ¿Cuál es su doctor?
Paciente: Con Dr. Jones.
Recepcionista: Llene esta forma, y firme aquí, por favor.
Paciente: Gracias. ¿Dónde está el baño?
Recepcionista: Sígueme, por favor.
Paciente: Gracias.
Recepcionista: ¿Trae su seguro médico?
Paciente: Sí.
Recepcionista: El doctor lo verá en un minuto. Siéntese, por favor.

C: ¿Cuándo es mi cita?: Practice scheduling appointments for the following dates.

1. May 9, 2014
2. July 1, 2016
3. October 4, 2015
4. December 13, 2014
5. January 19, 2016

D: ¿Cierto o falso?: Read each question and statement. If the response is appropriate and makes sense, write "cierto" (true). If the response does is not appropriate and does not make sense, write "falso" (false).

1. ¿Cuál es su número de póliza y grupo?
   uno, tres, siete, nueve, ocho, cero, dos, cinco, cero

2. ¿Trae su seguro médico?
   El doctor lo verá en un minuto.

3. ¿Dónde está el laboratorio?
   Su cita se ha cancelada.

4. ¿Dónde está la farmacia?
   Sígame, por favor.

5. ¿Tiene una cita hoy?
   Tengo una cita a las diez.

E: ¿Cuál respuesta?: Choose the most appropriate answer for the follow questions from the list:

A. Sígame, por favor.
B. Dr. Jones
C. Tengo una cita a las ocho.
D. tres, cuatro, seis, diez, nueve, dos, uno
E. Sí. Tengo seguro médico.

_____1. ¿Cuál es su número de póliza y grupo?

_____2. ¿Trae su seguro médico?

_____3. ¿Cuál es su doctor?

_____4. ¿Dónde está la farmacia?

_____5. ¿Tiene una cita hoy?

Did you know...

The Hispanic perception of time may be different than yours. In many Hispanic countries, people may not tend to be as punctual to certain events.. If invited to a party at 8:00, guests may not start arriving until 8:30 or later. In large cities, some events tend to run on schedule, and you shouldn't just assume that it is just ok to be late.

La historia médica
Medical History

Introducción

Taking the medical history of a patient can be very complex, however, the following questions can alert you to any problem areas that may take more time in questioning. You may want to turn to the "Specific Medical Areas" to ask further questions.

Do you have....?	¿Tiene......?
...chronic problems?	....problemas crónicas?
...problems with your heart?	...problemas con el corazón?
...problems with your ears?	...problemas con los oídos?
...problems with your kidneys?	...problemas con los riñones?
...problems with breathing?	...problemas con la respiración?
...problems with your stomach?	...problemas con el estómago?
...problems wit h your vision?	...problemas con la visión?
What is your blood type?	¿Cuál es su tipo de sangre?
Do you smoke?	¿Fuma usted?
Do you drink alcohol?	¿Toma usted alcohol?
Do you use drugs?	¿Usa usted drogas?
Do you have allergies?	¿Tiene alergias?
Have you ever been hospitalized?	¿Alguna vez ha estado hospitalizado?
When was the last time you recieved a tetanus shot?	¿Cuándo fue la última vez que recibió la vacuna antitetánica

¡Practica!

A. ¿Tiene problemas?: Ask if the patient has problems with the following areas according to the pictures.

1.

2.

3.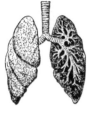

4.

5.

6.

B. ¿Cuáles problemas tiene usted?: Write out a question using the following vocabulary.

Example:
alergias - ¿Tiene alergias?

1. visión

2. alcohol

3. corazón

4. respiración

5. antitetánica

6. hospitalizado

C: ¿*Cómo se dice?*: Translate the following questions from English to Spanish.

1. Do you drink alcohol?

2. What is your blood type?

3. Do you have problems with your heart?

4. Do you use drugs?

5. Do you have allergies?

6. Do you have problems with vision?

7. Do you have problems breathing?

8. Do you smoke?

9. Have you ever been hospitalized?

10. Do you have problems with your ears?

Did you know...

There are several words used for the color brown depending what is described. "Marrón" describes man-made things; "castaño" describes eyes and hair; "pardo" describes things in nature; "café" covers a multitude of hues and is used as the general term.

Las síntomas

Symptoms

Introducción

The following phrases can be matched to form the needed question. Each of these questions should be answered with a "sí" (yes) or "no" (no). The word "tiene" can mean both *do you have* or *does s/he have* depending who it is refering to.

If you want to be more specific about who you are asking about, you may use:

Do you have...	¿Tiene usted...?
Does he have...	¿Tiene él...?
Does she have...	¿Tiene ella...?

Do you have.....	¿Tiene.........?
I have.......	Tengo.....
...chest pain	...dolor en el pecho
...difficulty breathing	...dificultad al respirar
...pain here	...dolor aquí
...diarrhea	...diarrea
...indigestion	...indigestión
...a stomach ache	...dolor de estómago
...constipation	...estreñimiento
...cramp	...calambres
...a backache	...dolor de espalda
...a headache	...dolor de cabeza
...a neck ache	...dolor en el cuello
...a cough	...tos

...an ear ache	...dolor en el oído
...a sore throat	...dolor en la garganta
...a rash	...una erupción
..something in my eye	...algo en el ojo
...vaginal discharge	...una secreción vaginal anormal
...fever	...fiebre
...chills	...escalofríos
...emotional problems	...problemas emocionales
...exhaustion	...agotamiento
...itching	...picazón
...severe pain	...dolores fuertes
...visual problems	...problemas de visión
Are you ill?	¿Está usted enfermo(a)?
Are you weak?	¿Está usted débil?
Are you bleeding?	¿Está usted sangrando?
Are you pregnant?	¿Está usted embarazada?
Are you nauseated?	¿Tiene usted náuseas?
Are you dizzy?	¿Está usted mareado(a)?
Are you hot?	¿Tiene usted calor?
Are you cold?	¿Tiene usted frío?
Are your lungs congested?	¿Tiene usted congestión en los pulmones?
I may have broken my (body part)	Me he roto ...(body part)
I have been raped.	Yo he sido violada.

I was bitten/stung by:	He sido picado por:
a dog/ cat	un perro/ gato
a bee	una abeja
a snake	una culebra/serpiente
an insect	un insecto
a spider	una araña

A conversar
¿Cuáles son las síntomas?

Conversación #1:

You are working with a woman who does not feel well. You are trying to figure out the symptoms that she is experiencing.

Conversación #2:

A child is complaining of a stomach ache. Try to find out what other symptoms the child is experiencing.

¡Practica!

A: Las traducciones: Match the Spanish phrases to their English translations.

_____1. dolor en la garganta   a. chest pain

_____2. algo en el ojo   b.constipation

_____3. dolor aquí   c. a rash

_____4. dolor de espalda   d. stomach ache

_____5. tos   e. pain here

_____6. ¿Está usted débil?   f. a neck ache

_____7. dolor de pecho   g. Are you bleeding?

_____8. ¿Tiene usted calor?   h. a cough

_____9. dolor de estómago   i. something in my eye

_____10. ¿Está usted mareado(a)?   j. a sore throat.

_____11. una erupción   k. Are you weak?

_____12. estreñimeinto   l. Are you dizzy?

_____13. ¿Está usted sangrando?   m. a backache

_____14. ¿Está usted embarazada?   n. Are you nauseated?

_____15. dolor en el oído   o. Are you hot?

_____16. ¿Tiene usted el estómago revuelto?   p. an ear ache

_____17. dolor en el cuello   q. Are you pregnant?

B: Más traducciones: Translate the following questions from Spanish to English.

1. Do you have a cough?

2. Do you have a fever?

3. Are you pregnant?

4. Are your lungs congested?

5. Do you have pain here?

6. Do you have a sore throat?

7. Does he have emotional problems?

8. Does she have difficulty breathing?

9. Does he have a headache?

10. Is she cold?

11. Is he hot?

12. Are you weak?

La enfermedad y la lesión
Illness and Injury

Introducción

The following questions identify specific symptoms of an injury or an illness. A few of the questions are more "open ended" so there are some choices for answers.

How do you feel?	¿Cómo se siente?
(Very) good.	(Muy) bien.
(Very) bad.	(Muy) mal.
Where does it hurt?	¿Dónde le duele?
When did your illness begin?	¿Cuándo empezó su enfermedad?
When did your pain begin?	¿Cuándo empezó el dolor?
last week	semana pasada
yesterday	ayer
today	hoy
How often?	¿Cada cuánto tiempo?
Every day/hour	Cada día/hora.
How long does it last?	¿Cuánto tiempo le dura?
___hour/___minutes	___hora/___minutos
Has it happened before?	¿Le ha pasado antes?
Have you thrown up?	¿Ha vomitado usted?
Did you have an accident?	¿Tuvo usted un accidente?
Where did it happen?	¿Dónde ocurrió?
When did it happen?	¿Cuándo ocurrió?

Have you ever had an operation?	¿Ha tenido alguna operación?
Have you ever been hospitalized?	¿Ha estado hospitalizadoalguna vez?
Are you taking any medications?	¿Está tomando alguna medicina?
Are you allergic to any medications?	¿Es alérgico a alguna medicina?
Do you have any valuables?	¿Tiene usted objetos de valor?
Do you have any scars?	¿Tiene usted cicatrices?
Do you have tattoos?	¿Tiene usted tatuajes?
We need to draw some blood from your arm.	Necesitamos tomar sangre de su brazo.
Do you want medication for the pain?	¿Quiere usted medicina para el dolor?
What is your blood type?	¿Cuál es su tipo de sangre?

**Note: The following statements can be asked as questions through changing the voice intonation.*

It is ….
…broken.
…burned.
…infected.
…inflamed.
…irritated.
…swollen.

Está…..
…roto.
…quemado.
…infectado.
…inflamado.
…irritado.
…hinchado.

Is your pain…?
…throbbing?
…sharp?
…constant?
…severe?
…burning?

¿Tiene un dolor…?
…pulsante?
…agudo?
….constante?
…muy fuerte?
…ardiendo?

¡Practica!

A: Un diálogo: Translate the following dialogue from Spanish to English.

Enfermera: Buenas noches. ¿Habla usted español?

Paciente: Buenas noches. Sí, hablo español.

Enfermera: ¿Cómo se siente?

Paciente: Muy mal.

Enfermera: ¿Dónde le duele?

Paciente: Me duele la cabeza.

Enfermera: ¿Cuándo empezó su enfermedad?

Paciente: Ayer, en la tarde.

Enfermera: ¿Cada cuánto tiempo?

Paciente: Cada 30 minutos.

Enfermera: ¿Le ha pasado antes?

Paciente: Sí. Dos veces.

Enfermera: ¿Ha vomitado usted?

Paciente: Sí.

Enfermera: ¿Tuvo usted un accidente?

Paciente: No.

Enfermera: ¿Está tomando alguna medicina?

Paciente: Si. Aspirina.

Enfermera: ¿Es alérgico a alguna medicina?

Paciente: Si, penicilina.

Enfermera: Gracias. El doctor lo verá en un minuto.

B: Dos diálogos: Translate the following dialogue from Spanish to English.

Recepcionista:	Buenos días. ¿Habla inglés?
Paciente:	No.
Recepcionista:	Hablo un poquito español. ¿En qué puedo ayudarle?
Paciente:	Quisiera ver al doctor.
Recepcionista:	¿Tiene una cita hoy?
Paciente:	Sí, tengo una cita con el doctor a las once.
Recepcionista:	¿Cómo se llama su doctor?
Paciente:	Dr. Smith.
Recepcionista:	¿Cómo se llama usted?
Paciente:	Me llamo Rafael Santos.
Recepcionista:	Llene esta forma, por favor.
Paciente:	Gracias.
Recepcionista:	De nada.
El paciente	llena la forma. (The patient fills out the form.)
Recepcionista:	Gracias.
Paciente:	De nada.
Recepctionista:	El doctor lo verá en un momento.
El paciente espera.	(Patient waits.)

Enfermera:	Buenos días Señor Santos. Me llamo Hazel.
Paciente:	Mucho gusto.
Enfermera:	Mucho gusto. ¿Cómo está?
Paciente:	Muy mal. Me duele.
Enfermera:	¿Dónde le duele?
Paciente:	Me duele la cabeza.
Enfermera:	¿Cuándo empezó la dolor?
Paciente:	Hoy. Por la mañana.
Enfermera:	¿Le ha pasado antes?
Paciente:	No.
Enfermera:	¿Está tomando alguna medicina?
Paciente:	Sí. Tomo Tylenol.
Enfermera:	¿Es alérgico a alguna medicina?
Paciente:	No.
Enfermera:	¿Tiene dolor en el pecho?
Paciente:	No.
Enfermera:	¿Tiene usted fiebre?
Paciente:	No.
Enfermera:	¿Tiene tos?
Paciente:	No.
Enfermera:	Ok. El doctor lo verá en un minuto.
Paciente:	Gracias.

Instrucciones para el paciente

Patient Instructions

Introducción

The following commands will help you communicate what you would like the patient to do. The commands that include parts of the body can be substituted with any body part.

Follow the instructions.	Siga las instrucciones.
Follow me.	Sígame.
Help me.	Ayúdeme.
Listen to the doctor.	Escuche al doctor.
Call me.	Llámame.
Look here.	Mire aquí.
Lower your head.	Baje la cabeza.
Raise your leg.	Levante la pierna.
Take my hand.	Tome mi mano.
Do it again.	Hágalo otra vez.
Breathe deeply.	Respire profundo.
Breathe slower	Respire más despacio
Close	Cierra
Open	Abra
Cough.	Tosa.
Do like I do.	Haga como yo.
Exhale.	Espire.
Inhale.	Aspire.

Get up.	Levántese.
Lay down.	Acuéstese.
Lay down on your left side.	Acuéstese a la izquierda.
Lay down on your right side.	Acuéstese a la derecha.
Lie down flat.	Acuéstese completamente.
Relax.	Relájese.
Sit.	Siéntese.
Take off your clothes.	Quítese la ropa.
Do not move.	No se mueva.
Point to where it hurts.	Indique dónde le duele.
Push	Empuje
Pull	Jale
Squeeze	Apriete
I need….	Necesito….
…a stool sample.	…una muestra del excremento.
…a urine sample.	…una muestra de la orina.
…a blood sample.	…una muestra de la sangre.
…a saliva sample.	…una muestra de la saliva.
Bend your arm.	Doble el brazo.
Move your leg.	Mueva la pierna.
Rest.	Descanse.
Turn.	Dale la vuelta.
Try to sleep.	Trate de dormir.

| Don't try to do too much. | No trate de hacer demasiado. |
| Calm down. | Cálmese. |

A conversar
¡Escuche al doctor!

Conversación #1:

You are working with a man who is feeling dizzy.
Give him instructions of what he should do.

Conversación #2:

You are working with an older woman who is having stomach problems. Give her directions as to what to do to get her prepared to see the doctor.

¡Practica!

A: Las traducciones: Translate the following words from Spanish to English or English to Spanish.

1. muestra de la orina

2. again

3. quítese la ropa

4. blood sample

5. muestra del excremento

6. breathe deeply

7. siéntese

8. close

9. a la derecha

10. cough

11. relájese

12. do like I do

13. abra

14. exhale

15. a la izquierda

16. get up

17. acuéstese

B: ¿Cómo se dice?: Match the English and Spanish translations.

1. Lay down on your left side.   a. Tosa.

2. Lay down on your right side.   b. Acuéstese completamente.

3. Take my hand.   c. Ayúdeme.

4. Look here.   d. Hágalo otra vez.

5. Lower your head.   e. Relájese.

6. Do not move.   f. Tome mi mano.

7. Move your leg.   g. Acuéstese a la derecha.

8. Cough.   h. Quítese la ropa.

9. Inhale.   i. Respire profundo.

10. Exhale.   j. Baje la cabeza.

11. Do it again.   k. Mueva la pierna.

12. Calm down.   l. Espire.

13. Relax.   m. Doble el brazo.

14. Breathe slower.   n. Mire aquí.

15. Lay down flat.   o. No se mueva.

16. Breathe deeply.   p. Cálmese.

17. Help me.   q. Acuéstese a la izquierda.

18. Follow me.   r. Respire más despacio.

19. Bend your arm.   s. Aspire.

20. Take off your clothes.   t. Sígame.

El cuarto del hospital

The Hospital Room

Introducción

Many times the "simple" items can be difficult to communicate. The following are a list of items found in a room of the hospital.

bed	cama
chair	silla
towel	toalla
washcloth	toallita para lavarse
cup	taza
straw	popote
lid	tapa
soap	jabón
pillow	almohada
cover	cobertor
food	comida
water	agua
ice	hielo
television	televisión
toothbrush	cepillo de dientes
bathroom	baño
mirror	espejo
toilet	inodoro

¡Practica!

A. En el hospital: Give the correct Spanish word for each fo the following objects.

1.

2.

3.

4.

5.

6.

B: ¿Qué necesito?: Tell what would be needed for the patient to do each of the following activities.

1. wash face

2. brush teeth

3. watch television

4. sleep

5. sit up

6. drink

7. eat

C: Las instrucciones: Practice giving the following directions to patients in Spanish.

1. Lay down on your right side and raise your arm.

2. Lay down flat and lower your head.

3. Sit and don't move.

4. Take off your clothes and lay down on your left side.

5. Move your arm and point to where it hurts.

Did you know...

If you need someone's attention, you may say "perdón" or "por favor". If they are further away, you may say "oiga" or "oye".

D: En el cuarto: Give the correct Spanish word for each of the following objects.

1.

2.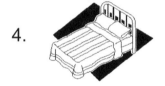

3.

4.

5.

6.

Las áreas médicas específicas

Specific Medical Areas

Introducción

Included on the following pages are Spanish vocabulary words for specific medical areas. The following areas are included:

*School Nurses
*Obstetrics & Gynecology
*Gastrointestinal/Abdominal/Genitourinary
*Cardiovascular
*Respiratory
*Burns
*Allergies
*Cancer
*Physical and Occupational Therapy
*Dietician
*Discussing Medication

School Nurses

I would like to see the nurse.	Quisiera ver la enfermera.
Do you have medical insurance?	¿Tiene seguro de médico?
What is your policy number and group number?	¿Cuál es su número de póliza y grupo?
Is your child included in the insurance?	¿Está incluido su niño en el seguro de medico?
You are going to have to wait a moment.	Va a tener que esperar un momento.
Fill out this form, please.	Llene esta forma, por favor.
Sign here.	Firme aquí.
You need to bring…..	Necesita traer…..
….the child's birth certificate.	….el certificado de nacimiento del niño/niña.

...the last physical exam report.	...el reporte del último examen físico.
...the vaccination report	...el reporte de todas las vacunas.
Come for your child. He/She has….	Venga por su niño/niña. El/ella tiene….
...lice.	….piojo.
...a fever.	….fiebre.
...a sickness.	….una enfermedad.
Please don't let your child return to school until they are fever free for 24 hours.	Por favor no deje su niño/a regresar a la escuela hasta que pase 24 horas sin fiebre.
How do you feel?	¿Cómo te sientes?
...sick	...enfermo
...afraid	...asustado/a
...angry	...enojado/a
...embarrassed	….avergonzado/a
...happy	...felíz
...frustrated	...frustrado/a
...lost	...perdido/a
...nervous	...nervioso/a
...sad	...triste
...tired	...cansado/a
...worried	...preocupado

Obstetrics & Gynecology

How many times have you been pregnant?	¿Cuántas veces ha estado embarazada?
How many children have you had?	¿Cuántos hijos ha tenido?
How close together are the pains?`	¿Cada cuánto le vienen los dolores?
Have you ever had twins?	¿Ha tenido gemelos?
Have you ever had forceps delivery?	¿Ha tenido un parta con fórceps?
Have you ever had a cesarean section?	¿Ha tenido una cesárea?
When was your last period?	¿Cuándo fue su última menstruación?
Breathe slowly through your mouth.	Respire lentamente por la boca.
Do you bleed in between periods?	¿Usted sangra entre menstruaciones?
Do you have heavy or light flow?	¿Sale poca o mucha sangre?
foam and condom	espuma y condón
Have you had vaginal bleeding?	¿Ha salido sangre por vagina?
Have you ruptured your membranes?	¿Se ha rota la fuente?
I need to do a vaginal exam.	Necesito examinar su vagina.
I need to examine your breasts.	Necesito examinar los pechos.
Do you want your baby circumcised?	¿Quiere que su bebe sea circunciso?
labor pains	contracciones o dolores del parto
miscarriage/spontaneous abortion	aborto natural, involuntario
period	regla o menstruación
Please slide closer to the edge of the table.	Acérquesea la orilla del borde de la mesa.
Please stand up/lie down.	Levántese/Acuéstese por favor.

pregnancy	el embarazo
When was the first day of your last period?	¿Cuándo fue el primer día de su última menstruación?
Put your legs up here.	Por favor, ponga las piernas aquí.
rape	violación
oral contraceptive pill	la pastilla
voluntary abortion	aborto voluntario
Try to relax your muscles.	Trate de relajar los músculos.
When did the pains start?	¿Cuándo empezaron los dolores?
When is your due date?	¿Cuál es la fecha de parto?
Do you want to breast feed?	¿Usted desea amamantar?
Do you want to bottle feed?	¿Usted desea dar alimento con biberón?
Do you want something to alleviate the pain?	¿Quiere usted algo para aliviar el dolor?
IV	Método Intravenoso
Lamaze or Natural Method	Lamaze o metodo natural
Epidural	Anestesia Epidural
Epidural Block	Bloqueo Epidural
Pudental	Anestesia Vaginal
Concentrate your attention on your breathing.	Concentra su atención en su respiración.
Sit at the edge of the bed with your back arched.	Siéntese a la orilla al borde de la cama con la espalda arqueada.
premature baby	bebé prematuro
prenatal care	cuidado prenatal

pelvic exam	examen pélvico
labor	trabajo del parto
placenta	placenta
cervical cancer	cáncer cervical
folic acid	ácido fólico
push	empuje
heartburn	acides
dehydration	deshidratación
birth control pills	las píldoras anticonceptivas
creams	las cremas
diaphragm	el diafragma
douching	el lavado vaginal
IUD	el aparato intrauterino
rhythm method	el método del ritmo
tubal ligation	la ligadura de los tubos
vasectomy	la vasectomía
embryo	el embrión
fetus	el feto
intercourse	la relaciones sexuales
menstrual cycle	el ciclo menstrual
You are pregnant.	Está embarazada.
You need a …..	Necesita un……
…enema	…enema
…pap smear	…examen de papanicolaou

…pelvic exam	…examen pélvico
…pregnancy test	…examen de embarazo
…rectal exam	…examen del recto
…Rh factor test	…examen del factor Rhesus del sangre
…urine test	…examen de orina
Did you ever have a miscarriage?	¿Perdió un bebé alguna vez?
Do you have other children?	¿Tiene otros hijos?
birth defect	defecto de nacimiento
blind	ciego
deaf	sordo
fetal alcohol syndrome	el síndrome de alcohol fetal
jaundice	ictericia
miscarriage	una pérdida
premature	prematuro
still born	nacido muerto
pacifier	el chupete
colic	el cólico
diaper	el pañal
nap	siesta
talcum powder	el talco de bebe

Did you know...

Religion has traditionally played a large role in the Hispanic world. Even secular activities may begin with a mass or religious ceremony such as with a military parade, various types of celebrations, or fishing fleets.

Genitourinary

Do you have:	¿Tiene usted....?
constipation	estreñimiento
diarrhea	diarrea
gallstones	cálculos biliares
gonorrhea	gonorrea
heart burn	acides
hemorrhoids	hemorroides
hepatitis	hepatitis
indigestion	indigestión
jaundice	ictericia
nausea	náusea
blood in the urine	sangre en la orina
stomach ache	dolor de estómago
syphilis	sífilis
ulcers	ulceras
venereal disease	enfermedadvenérea
vomiting	vómito
Does it hurt when I press here?	¿Le duele cuando yo pongo presión aquí?
Do you have regular bowels?	¿Es regular su excremento?
Has this ever happened before?	¿Ha ocurrido esto antes?

How many alcoholic beverages do you drink a day?	¿Cuántas bebidas alcohólicas toma cada día?
How many bottles of pop do you drink a day?	¿Cuántas botellas de refresco toma cada día?
How many cups of coffee do you drink a day?	¿Cuántas tazas de café toma cada día?
How many glasses of water do you drink a day?	¿Cuántos vasos de agua toma cada día?
How many glasses of milk do you drink a day?	¿Cuántos vasos de leche toma cada día?
Is there any food you cannot eat?	¿Hay alguna comida que no puede comer?
Have you had….?	¿Ha tenido….?
…an enema?	…un enema de bario?
…constipation?	….estreñimiento?
…diarrhea?	…diarrea?
…a stomach illness?	…alguna enfermedad gastrointestinal?
…heartburn?	…ardor en el estómago?
…hemorrhoids?	…hemorroides?
…hiccups?	…hipo?
…parasites in the stool?	…parásitos en el excremento?
…ulcers?	…úlceras?

Cardiovascular

Do you have chest pain?	¿Tiene usted dolor en el pecho?
Where does it hurt?	¿Dónde le duele usted?
When did it start?	¿Cuándo empezó?
Does the pain radiate?	¿Radia el dolor?
Have you ever had a hear attack?	¿Ha tenido alguna vez un ataque de corazón?
Do you have a history of heart problems?	¿Tiene un historia de problemas del corazón?
Do you have:	¿Tiene usted....?
palpitations	palpitaciones
murmur	murmullo en el corazón
shortness of breath	falta de aire
hypertension	presión alta
Has this ever happened before?	¿Ha ocurrido esto antes?
stroke	apoplejía, derrame cerebral, o ataque
natural pacemaker	marcapaso natural
artificial pacemaker	marcapaso artificial
tube for groin	tubo para la ingle
These will bleed if you move your waist or your leg.	Estas cosas va a sangrar si mueve su cintura o su pierna.
blood pressure (high/low)	presión sanguínea (alto/bajo)
rhythm of the heart	ritmo del corazón
atrium	aurícula

ventricle	ventrículo
catheter	catéter
implantation	implantación
local anesthetic	anestésico local
coronary artery	arteria coronaria
blocks	bloqueados
heartburn	cardialgia
dehydration	deshidratación
Do you sleep well?	¿Duerme bien?
Do you wake up at night with shortness of breath and perspiring?	¿Despierta por la noche con la respiración corta y sudando?
Do you get short of breath upon exercise?	¿Se queda sin aliento después de hacer un esfuerzo?
heartbeat	el ritmo cardíaco
hypertension	la hipertensión arterial
You are overweight.	Tiene el sobrepeso.
The artery is blocked.	La arteria está obstruida.
The heart muscles are strained.	Los músculos del corazón están forzados.
Your pulse is very fast.	Su pulso está muy rápido.

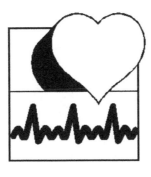

Respiratory

Do you have:	¿Tiene usted.....?
a cold	un catarro
asthma	asma
chronic bronchitis	bronquitis crónica
cough	tos
difficulty breathing	dificultad para respirar
difficulty breathing at night	dificultad en respirar por la noche
dry cough	tos seca
emphysema	enfisema
expiration	con expiración
flu	gripe
heart disease	enfermedades de corazón
heart failure	falla cardiaca
phlegm	flema
pneumonia	neumonia
sore throat	dolor de garganta
cough with aspiration	tos con aspiración
bronchial asthma	asma bronquial
bronchopneumonia	bronconeumonia
Has this ever happened before?	¿Ha ocurrido esto antes?

Burns

What caused the burn?	¿Qué causó la quemadura?
Fire	fuego
hot water	agua caliente
chemicals	químicos
electricity	electricidad
Did you inhale any smoke?	¿Inhaló humo?
Do you have difficulty breathing?	¿Tiene usted dificultad para respirar?
Is the pain severe?	¿Es severo el dolor?
First, second, third degree	primer, segundo, tercer grado

Allergies

What are you allergic to?	¿A qué es alérgico/a?
nothing	nada
penicillin	penicilina
certain foods	ciertas comidas
insect stings	picaduras de insectos
Were you stung by a bee?	¿Ha sido picado por una abeja?
Has this ever happened before?	¿Ha ocurrido esto antes?
Have you inhaled anything unusual?	¿Ha ingerido algo extraño?
Have you ingested anything unusual?	¿Ha tomado algo extraño?
Does your skin itch?	¿Tiene picazón?
Do you have asthma?	¿Tiene asma?

Cancer

cancer	el cáncer
cancerous	canceroso
chemotherapy	quimioterapia
mammograms	monogramas
breast	seno
to smoke	fumar
stop smoking	dejar de fumar
radiology	radioterapia
treatment	tratamiento
leukemia	la leukemia
monthly self exam	examen mensual
biopsy	biopsia
hormonal therapy	terapia de hormonas
He/she/you are going to…	El/ella/usted va a ….
…feel tired and weak.	…sentirse cansado y débil.
…to have nausea, vomiting, diarrhea, and constipation.	…tener náuseas, vómitos, diarrea y estreñimiento.
…lose your hair and the color of your skin.	…perder el pelo y el color de la piel.
We found…	Encontramos…
…an abnormality.	…una anormalidad.
…a bump.	…una hinchachazón.
…a cyst.	…un quiste.

…a lesion.	…una llaga.
…a lump.	…un bulto.
…a spot.	…una mancha.
…a tumor.	…un tumor.
The doctor needs a biopsy of your___.	El médico necesita una biopsia de su ___.
When we receive the results, we will know what to do.	Cuando recibamos los resultas, sabremos qué hacer.

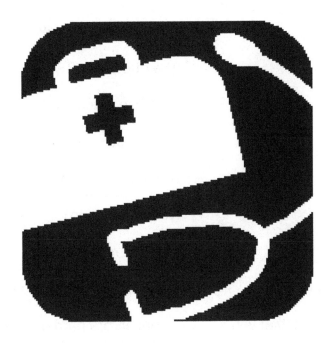

Physical and Occupational Therapy

Are there ramps?	¿Hay rampas?
Are there elevators?	¿Hay elevadores?
Are you comfortable?	¿Está cómodo?
Can you get out of bed?	¿Puede bajar de la cama?
Can you read?	¿Puede leer?
Can you write?	¿Puede escribir?
Did you fall?	¿Se cayó?
Do you need help?	¿Necesita ayuda?
Do you remember me?	¿Se acuerda de mí?
Does this hurt?	¿Le duele esto?
Sit down.	Siéntese usted.
Stand up.	Levántese usted.
Breathe regularly.	Respire regularmente.
Don't be afraid.	No tenga miedo.
One more time.	Una vez más.
You must be very careful.	Tiene que tener mucho cuidado.
I will watch to make sure that you can do it correctly.	La observaré para estar seguro que usted puede hacerlo correctamente.
That is right.	Está bien.
I'm finished.	Ya terminé.
Do you wear glasses?	¿Usted usa lentes?
Follow my finger.	Siga mi dedo.

Look up.	Mire para arriba.
Look down.	Mire para abajo.
Do you have a hearing aide?	¿Tiene usted un aparato para oír?
I am going to check your arm.	Voy a revisar su brazo.
Please do this.	Por favor haga esto.
Lift your arms.	Levante los brazos.
Flex your arm and don't let me move it.	Doble el brazo y no me dejes doblar.
Bend your elbow.	Doble el codo.
Now the other.	Ahora el otro.
Place your arms behind your head.	Pon las manos detrás de la cabeza.
Place your arms behind your back.	Pon los brazos atrás.
Bend the wrist.	Doble la muñeca.
Squeeze my hand.	Apriete mi mano.
Close your hand.	Cierre la mano.
Who helps you at home?	¿Quién le ayuda en casa?
Do you have dentures?	¿Tiene usted dentaduras?
Look at me.	Míreme.
How long have you felt this way?	¿Desde cuándo se siente así?
cane	bastón
crutches	muletas
wheel chair	silla de ruedas

Dietician

diabetes	diabetes
too high	demasiado alto
too low	demasiado bajo
potassium	potasio
phosphorus	fósforo
protein	proteína
sodium/ salt	sal
fluids	fluidos
dangerous for…..	Hace daño por…
You should not eat….	No debe comer…
You can eat….	Puede comer…
You should eat….	Debe comer…
You can drink….	Puede beber….
Juice	jugo de…
fruit	fruta
apples	manzanas
oranges	naranjas
kiwi	kiwi
cantaloupe	melón
grapes	uvas
watermelon	sandía

grapefruit	toronja
bananas	plátanos
prunes	ciruelas secas
strawberries	fresas
vegetables	legumbres
tomatoes	tomates
beans	frijoles
corn	maíz
broccoli	brócoli
onions	cebolla
potatos	papas
beets	remolacha
spinach	espinaca
squash	calabaza
sweet potatos	batatas
carrots	zanahorias
peas	guisantes
lettuce	lechuga
green beans	habichuelas verdes
milk	leche
cheese	queso
hot chocolate	chocolate caliente
ice cream	helado

cottage cheese	requesón
yogurt	yogur
meat	carne
beef	carne de res/ vaca
turkey	pavo
chicken	pollo
fish	pescado
eggs	huevos
pork	puerco

Did you know...

Business is conducted on a more personal level than in our culture. It is common for a conversation to shift back and fourth from personal to business matters. Being strictly "businesslike" may be a turn off to those in the Hispanic world.

Medication

Do you take…?
You need to take…

¿Toma…?
Necesita tomar…

analgesic	analgésico
antacid	antiácido
antihemorrhagic	antihemorrágico
antihistamine	antihistamínico
apirin	aspirina
barbiturates	barbitúricos
castor oil	aceite de ricino
cocaine	cocaína
codeine	codeína
contraceptive	contraceptiva
cough drops	pastillas para la tos
diuretic	diurético
epson salts	sal de higuera
estrogen	estrógeno
expectorant	expectorante
heroin	heroína
hormones	hormonas
iodine	yodo
laxative	laxante
lozenges	pastillas de chupar
magnesia	magnesia
milk of magnesia	leche de magnesia
morphine	morfina
narcotic	narcótico
novocain	novocaína
penicillin	penicilina
sedatives	sedantes
stimulant	estimulante
sulfa	sulfa
suppository	supositorio
tranquilizer	tranquilizante
vaccine	vacuna
vitamins	vitaminas

El glosario

The Glossary

"You can easily find all of the vocabulary words in this manual. They are alphabetized in a Spanish to English, and English to Spanish dictionary."

English to Spanish Glossary

above	arriba de	blood	sangre *(f.)*
accident	accidente *(m.)*	blue	azul
address	dirección *(f.)*	bored	aburrido/a
administrator	administrador/a *(m./f.)*	boyfriend	novio *(m.)*
after	después	brain	cerebro *(m.)*
afternoon, late	tarde *(f.)*	bread	pan *(m.)*
age	edad *(f.)*	breakfast	desayuno *(m.)*
allergy	alergia *(f.)*	breathe	respire
also	también	bring *(to)*	traer
analgesic	analgésico *(m.)*	broccoli	brócoli *(m.)*
and	y	broken	roto
angry	enojado/a	brother	hermano *(m.)*
answer	contesta *(f.)*	brother in law	cuñado *(m.)*
answer	respuesta *(f.)*	brown	café
answer *(to)*	contestar	burned	quemado
antacid	antiácido *(m.)*	burning	ardiendo
antihemorrhagic	antihemorrágico *(m.)*	bus driver	conductor/a *(m./f.)*
antihistamine	antihistamínico *(m.)*	butter	mantequilla *(f.)*
apirin	aspirina *(f.)*	buy *(to)*	comprar
apples	manzanas *(f.)*	cafeteria	cafetería *(f.)*
appointment	cita *(f.)*	cake	pastel *(m.)*
April	abril	cake/sandwich	torta *(f.)*
arm	brazo *(m.)*	calendar	calendario *(m.)*
arrive *(to)*	llegar	call *(to)*	llamar
article	artículo *(m.)*	calm down	cálmese
artistic	artístico/a	candy	dulces *(m.)*
ask *(to)*	preguntar	cantaloupe	melón *(m.)*
asparagus	espárrago *(m.)*	carrots	zanahorias *(f.)*
association	asociación *(f.)*	carry, wear *(to)*	llevar
athletic	atlético/a	cash	dinero en efectivo *(m.)*
auditorium	auditorio *(m.)*	castor oil	aceite de ricino *(m.)*
August	agosto	cat	gato/a *(m./f.)*
aunt	tía *(f.)*	celery	apio *(m.)*
aunts and uncles	tíos *(m.)*	cell phone	teléfono celular *(m.)*
awake	despierto	cent(s)	centavo(s) *(m.)*
back	espalda *(f.)*	cereal	cereal *(m.)*
bacon	tocino *(m.)*	ceremony	ceremonia *(f.)*
bad	mal	chair	silla *(f.)*
bananas	plátanos *(m.)*	change	cambio *(m.)*
barbituates	bartitúricos *(m.)*	change *(to)*	cambiar
bathroom	baño *(m.)*	cheese	queso *(m.)*
bathroom	baño *(m.)*	cherry	cereza *(f.)*
be *(to)*	estar	chicken	pollo *(m.)*
be *(to)*	ser	chills	escalofríos *(m.)*
be pleasing/to like *(to)*	gustar	chocolate	chocolate *(m.)*
bed	cama *(f.)*	class	clase *(f.)*
bee	abeja *(f.)*	client	cliente *(m/f)*
beef	carne de res *(m.)*	clinic	clínica *(f.)*
beer	cerveza *(f.)*	close	cierra
before	antes	close *(to)*	cerrar
behind	detrás de	coach	entrenador/a *(m./f.)*
believe *(to)*	creer	cocaine	cocaína *(f.)*
bend	doble	codeine	codeína *(f.)*
beside	al lado de	coffee	café *(m.)*
between	entre	coin	moneda *(f.)*
big	grande	cold	frío *(m.)*
bill	billete *(m.)*	come *(to)*	venir
birth certificate	certificado de nacimiento *(m.)*	common	común
bitten	picado	comprehension	comprensión *(f.)*
black	negro	computer lab	laboratorio de computadoras *(m.)*
bleed *(to)*	sangrar	condiments	condimentos *(m.)*
bleeding	sangrando	congestion	congestión *(f.)*
blessed	bendito	consonant	consonante *(m.)*

English to Spanish Glossary

constant	constante	eighty five	ochenta y cinco
constipation	estreñimiento (m.)	eighty four	ochenta y cuatro
contraceptive	anticonceptivo (m.)	eighty nine	ochenta y nueve
conversation	conversación (f.)	eighty one	ochenta y uno
converse (to)	conversar	eighty seven	ochenta y siete
cookie	galleta (f.)	eighty six	ochenta y sies
corn	maíz (m.)	eighty three	ochenta y tres
cost	cuesta	eighty two	ochenta y dos
cough	tos (m.)	eleven	once
cough (command)	tosa	enter (to)	entrar
cough drops	pastillas para la tos (f.)	epson salts	sal de higuera (f.)
counseling office	oficina del consejero/a (f.)	estrogen	estrugeno (m.)
counselor	consejero/a (m./f.)	excited	emocionado/a
courtesy	cortesía (f.)	excuse me	con permiso
cousin (f)	prima (f.)	exhale	espire
cousin (m)	primo (m.)	exhaustion	agotamiento (m.)
cousins	primos (m.)	expectorant	expectorante (m.)
cover	cobertor (m.)	explanation	explicación (f.)
covered	cubierto	express (to)	expresar
cramp	crampa (f.)	expression	expresión (f.)
cramps	calambres (m.)	extroverted	extrovertido/a
cream	crema (f.)	eye	ojo (m.)
cucumber	pepino (m.)	face	cara (f.)
culture	cultura (f.)	fall (to)	caer
cup	taza (f.)	family	familia (f.)
currency	moneda (f.)	family tree	árbol genealógico (m.)
custodian	guardián/a (m./f.)	famous	famoso/a
cut (to)	cortar	far, far from	lejos de
dairy	lateo (m.)	farewell	despedida (f.)
dance (to)	bailar	fat	gordo/a
dark complected	moreno/a	father	padre (m.)
date	fecha (f.)	father in law	suegro (m.)
daughter	hija (f.)	February	febrero
day	día (m.)	fever	fiebre (f.)
dead	muerto	fever	fiebre (f.)
December	diciembre	fifteen	quince
decide (to)	decidir	fifty	cincuenta
dentist	dentista (m/f)	fifty eight	cincuenta y ocho
desire (to)	desear	fifty five	cincuenta y cinco
desserts	postres (m.)	fifty four	cincuenta y cuatro
dialogue	diálogo (m.)	fifty nine	cincuenta y nueve
diarrhea	diarrea (f.)	fifty one	cincuenta y uno
dime	diez centavos (m.)	fifty seven	cincuenta y siete
dinner	cena (m.)	fifty six	cincuenta y sies
discovered	descubierto	fifty three	cincuenta y tres
diuretic	diurético (f.)	fifty two	cincuenta y dos
divorced	divorciado/a	fight (to)	luchar
dizzy	mareado/a	find (to)	encontrar
do, make (to)	hacer	finger	dedo (m.)
doctor	doctor/a (m./f.)	fingernail	uña (f.)
dog	perro/a (m./f.)	finish (to)	terminar
dollar (s)	dólar(es) (m.)	fireman	bombero (m.)
done, made	hecho	fish	pescado (m.)
drink (to)	beber	five	cinco
drinks	bebidas (f.)	five hundred	quinientos
drug	droga (f.)	fly (to)	volar
eat (to)	comer	follow (to)	seguir
eggs	huevos (m.)	follow me	sígame
eight	ocho	food	comida (f.)
eight hundred	ochocientos	foolish	tonto/a
eighteen	dieciocho	foot	pie (m.)
eighty	ochenta	forget (to)	olvidar
eighty eight	ochenta y ocho	form	forma (f.)

English to Spanish Glossary

formal	formal *(m.)*	help *(to)*	ayudar
forty	cuarenta	help me	ayúdeme
four	cuatro	here	aquí
four hundred	cuatrocientos	heroin	heroina *(f.)*
fourteen	catorce	holiday	día festivo *(m.)*
fourty eight	cuarenta y ocho	homework	tarea *(f.)*
fourty five	cuarenta y cinco	hormones	hormonas *(f.)*
fourty four	cuarenta y cuatro	hospital	hospital *(m.)*
fourty nine	cuarenta y nueve	hot	calor *(m.)*
fourty one	cuarenta y uno	hot dog	perro caliente *(m.)*
fourty seven	cuarenta y siete	hour	hora *(f.)*
fourty six	cuarenta y seis	how much	cuánto(s)
fourty three	cuarenta y tres	how/what	cómo
fourty two	cuarenta y dos	hundred	cien
French	francés *(m.)*	hurt	duele
Friday	viernes *(m.)*	husband	esposo *(m.)*
fried	frito	husband	marido *(m.)*
friend	amigo/a *(m./f.)*	I	yo
friendly	amable	ice	hielo *(m.)*
frightened	asustado/a	ice cream	helado *(m.)*
fruit	fruta *(f.)*	identification	identificación *(f.)*
frustrated	frustrado/a	in front of, facing	enfrente de
funny	cómico/a	in, on	en
gender	género *(m.)*	indicate *(to)*	indicar
get up	levenatese	indigestion	indigestión *(f.)*
girlfriend	novia *(f.)*	infected	infectado
give *(to)*	dar	inflamed	inflamado
good	bien	informal	informal *(m.)*
good afternoon	buenas tardes	information	información *(f.)*
good evening	buenas noches	informed	informado
good morning	buenos días	inhale	aspire
good-bye	adiós	inner ear	oído *(m.)*
good-looking	guapo/a	insect	insecto *(m.)*
grab *(to)*	agarrar	inside	dentro de
grandchildren	nietos *(m.)*	instructions	instrucciones *(f.)*
granddaughter	nieta *(f.)*	insurance	seguro *(m.)*
grandfather	abuelo *(m.)*	intelligent	inteligente
grandmother	abuela *(f.)*	interpret *(to)*	interpretar
grandparents	abuelos *(m.)*	introduction	introducción *(f.)*
grandson	nieto *(m.)*	introduction, presentation	presentación *(f.)*
grapefruit	toronja *(f.)*	invite *(to)*	invitar
grapes	uvas *(f.)*	iodine	yodo *(m.)*
gray	gris	it	lo
green	verde	itching	picazón *(f.)*
green beans	judía verde *(f.)*	January	enero
greeting	saludo *(m.)*	jello	gelatina *(f.)*
gymnasium	gimnasio *(m.)*	juice	jugo *(m.)*
hair	pelo *(m.)*	July	julio
half	media *(f.)*	June	junio
ham	jamón *(m.)*	ketchup	kétchup *(m.)*
hamburger	hamburguesa *(f.)*	know (a fact) *(to)*	saber
hand	mano *(f.)*	know (a person/place) *(to)*	conocer
happy	alegre	laboratory	laboratorio *(m.)*
have *(to)*	tener	laxative	laxante *(m.)*
have breakfast *(to)*	desayunar	lay down	acuéstese
have dinner *(to)*	cenar	learn *(to)*	aprender
have lunch *(to)*	almorzar	leave *(to)*	salir
he	él	leave behind *(to)*	dejar
head	cabeza *(f.)*	left	izquierda *(f.)*
healthy	sano/a	leg	pierna *(f.)*
hear *(to)*	oír	less	menos
heart	corazón *(m.)*	letter	carta *(f.)*
hello	hola	lettuce	lechuga *(f.)*

English to Spanish Glossary

librarian	bibliotecario/a *(m./f.)*	next	próximo *(m.)*
library	biblioteca *(f.)*	nice	simpático/a
lice	piojo *(m.)*	nickel	cinco centavos *(m.)*
lid	tapa *(f.)*	niece	sobrina *(f.)*
light complected	rubio/a	nieces and nephews	sobrinos *(m.)*
lip	labio *(m.)*	night	noche *(f.)*
listen	escuche	nine	nueve
listen to *(to)*	escuchar	nine hundred	novecientos
little	poco	nineteen	diecinueve
live *(to)*	vivir	ninety	noventa
location	locación *(f.)*	ninety eight	noventa y ocho
look	mire	ninety five	noventa y cinco
look for, search *(to)*	buscar	ninety four	noventa y cuatro
lose *(to)*	perder	ninety nine	noventa y nueve
lost	perdido/a	ninety one	noventa y uno
love (things) *(to)*	encantar	ninety seven	noventa y siete
love *(to)*	amar	ninety six	noventa y seis
lower	baje	ninety three	noventa y tres
lower *(to)*	bajar	ninety two	noventa y dos
lozenges	pastillas de chupar *(f.)*	no	no
lunch	almuerzo *(m.)*	none	ninguna
magnesia	magnesia *(f.)*	noon	mediodía *(m.)*
man	hombre *(m.)*	nose	nariz *(f.)*
March	marzo	nothing	nada
marital status	estado civil *(m.)*	noun	sustantivo *(m.)*
married	casado/a	November	noviembre
materials	materiales *(f.)*	novocain	novocaína *(f.)*
May	mayo	numbers	números *(m.)*
mayonnaise	mayonesa *(f.)*	nurse	enfermera *(f.)*
meals	repas *(f.)*	nurse	enfermero/a *(m./f.)*
mean	antipático/a	nurse's office	oficina del enfermero/a *(f.)*
meat	carne *(f.)*	October	octubre
medical insurance	seguro de médico *(m.)*	of, from	de
medicine	medicina *(f.)*	official	oficial *(m.)*
medium	mediano/a	old	viejo/a
midnight	medianoche *(f.)*	on top of	encima de
mile	milla *(f.)*	one	uno
milk	leche *(f.)*	onion	cebolla *(f.)*
milk of magnesia	leche de magnesia *(f.)*	open *(command)*	abra
million	millón	open *(to)*	abrir
minute	minuto *(m.)*	opened	abierto
mirror	espejo *(m.)*	operation	operación *(f.)*
Miss	señorita *(f.)*	orange	anaranjado
molar	muela *(f.)*	oranges	naranjas *(f.)*
moment	momento *(m.)*	outer ear	oreja *(f.)*
Monday	lunes *(m.)*	outside of	fuera de
money	dinero *(m.)*	pain	dolor *(m.)*
month	mes *(m.)*	paint *(to)*	pintar
more	más	pancake	panqueque *(m.)*
morphine	morfina *(f.)*	para	asistente *(m./f.)*
mother	madre *(f.)*	parents	padres *(m.)*
mother in law	suegra *(f.)*	part	parte *(f.)*
mouth	boca *(f.)*	party	fiesta *(f.)*
move	mueva	pass *(to)*	pasar
Mr., sir	señor *(m.)*	pasta	pasta *(f.)*
Mrs., ma'am	señora *(f.)*	patient	paciente *(m/f)*
much, a lot	mucho	peach	durazno *(m.)*
mustard	mostaza *(f.)*	pears	peras *(f.)*
narcotic	narcótico *(m.)*	peas	arvejas *(f.)*
nauseated	náuseas	penicillin	penicilina *(f.)*
near, close to	cerca de	penny	un centavo *(m.)*
neck	cuello *(m.)*	pepper	pimienta *(f.)*
nephew	sobrino *(m.)*	pharmacy	farmacia *(f.)*

English to Spanish Glossary

pillow	almohada (f.)	secretion	secreción (f.)
pink	rosado	section	sección (f.)
play (to)	jugar	security guard	guardia de seguridad (m./f.)
please	por favor	sedatives	sedantes (m.)
police	policía (m/f)	see (to)	ver
popular	popular	seen	visto
pork	cerdo (m.)	sell (to)	vender
potato	papa (f.)	seller	vendedor (m.)
practice	práctica (f.)	sentence	frase (f.)
practice (to)	practicar	sentence	oración (f.)
prefer (to)	preferir	September	septiembre
pregnant	embarazada	serious	serio/a
prepare (to)	preparar	seven	siete
prepared	preparado/a	seven hundred	setecientos
pretty	bonito/a	seventeen	diecisiete
principal	director/a (m./f.)	seventy	setenta
principal, director	director (m.)	seventy eight	setenta y ocho
pronunciation	pronunciación (f.)	seventy five	setenta y cinco
psychologist	psicólogo/a (m./f.)	seventy four	setenta y cuatro
pull	jale	seventy nine	setenta y nueve
purple	morado	seventy one	setenta y uno
push	empuje	seventy seven	setenta y siete
put (to)	poner	seventy six	setenta y seis
quarter	cuarto (m.)	seventy three	setenta y tres
quarter	veinticinco centavos (m.)	seventy two	setenta y dos
question	pregunta (f.)	sharp	agudo
radio	radio (f.)	she	ella
rain (to)	llover	shopping	compras (f.)
raise	levante	short	bajo/a
raise (to)	levantar	should, owe (to)	deber
rash	erupción (f.)	shout (to)	gritar
reaction	reacción (f.)	show (to)	mostrar
read (to)	leer	shower	ducha (f.)
reason	razón (f.)	siblings	hermanos (m.)
receive (to)	recibir	sick	enfermo/a
reception	recepción (f.)	sickness	enfermedad (f.)
receptionist	recepcionista (f.)	sickness	enfermedad (f.)
receptionist	recepcionista (m./f.)	sing (to)	cantar
recommend (to)	recomendar	single	soltero/a
red	rojo	sister	hermana (f.)
red headed	pelirrojo/a	sister in law	cuñada (f.)
relax	relájese	sit down	sientese
repeat	repite	situation	situación (f.)
repeat (to)	repetir	six	seis
request, ask for (to)	pedir	six hundred	seiscientos
resolve (to)	resolver	sixteen	dieciséis
rest	descanse	sixty	sesenta
return (to)	regresar	sixty eight	sesenta y ocho
right	derecha (f.)	sixty five	sesenta y cinco
roast beef	rosbif (m.)	sixty four	sesenta y cuatro
run (to)	correr	sixty nine	sesenta y nueve
sad	triste	sixty one	sesenta y uno
said	dicho	sixty seven	sesenta y siete
saliva	saliva (f.)	sixty six	sesenta y seis
salt	sal (f.)	sixty three	sesenta y tres
sample	muestra	sixty two	sesenta y dos
sandwich	sándwich (m.)	sleep (to)	dormir
satisfied	satisfecho	slowly	despacio
Saturday	sábado (m.)	small	pequeño/a
sausage	salchicha (f.)	smoke (to)	fumar
say, tell (to)	decir	snake	culebra (f.)
scars	cicatrices (f.)	snake	serpiente (m.)
search	búsqueda (f.)	snow (to)	nevar

English to Spanish Glossary

soap	jabón (m.)	thirty eight	treinta y ocho
soft drink	refresco (m.)	thirty five	treinta y cinco
some	alguna	thirty four	treinta y cuatro
something	algo (m.)	thirty nine	treinta y nueve
son	hijo (m.)	thirty one	treina y uno
sons and daughters	hijos (m.)	thirty seven	treinta y siete
so-so	así así	thirty six	treinta y seis
sound	sonido (m.)	thirty three	treina y tres
spaghetti	espagueti (m.)	thirty two	treinta y dos
speak (to)	hablar	this	este/a
spider	araña (f.)	those	esos/as
spouses	esposos (m.)	those over there	aquellos/as
squash	calabaza (f.)	thousand	mil
stay (to)	quedar	three	tres
steak	bistec (m.)	three hundred	trescientos
stepbrother	hermanastro (m.)	throat	garganta (f.)
stepdaughter	hijastra (f.)	throbbing	pulsante
stepfather	padrastro (m.)	Thursday	jueves (m.)
stepmother	madrastra (f.)	timid	tímido/a
stepsister	hermanastra (f.)	tired	cansado/a
stepson	hijastro (m.)	to him, her, you	le
stimulant	estimulante (m.)	to, at	a
stomach	estómago (m.)	today	hoy
stool	escremento (m.)	toilet	inodoro (m.)
straight ahead	derecho	tomato	tomate (m.)
straw	popote (m.)	tomorrow, morning	mañana
strawberries	fresas (f.)	tongue	lengua (f.)
strong	fuerte	tooth	diente (m.)
strong	fuerte	toothbrush	cepillo de dientes (m.)
student	estudiante (m/f)	touch, play (instrument) (to)	tocar
study (to)	estudiar	towel	toalla (f.)
sugar	azúcar (m.)	tradition	tradición (f.)
sulfa	sulfa (f.)	tranquilizer	tranquilizante (m.)
Sunday	domingo (m.)	translate (to)	traducir
suppository	supositorio (m.)	translation	traducción (f.)
swim (to)	nadar	travel (to)	viajar
swollen	hinchado	truth	verdad (f.)
syllable	sílaba (f.)	Tuesday	martes (m.)
take	tome	turkey	pavo (m.)
take (to)	tomar	tv	tele (f.)
talented	talentoso/a	twelve	doce
tall	alto/a	twenty	veinte
tattoos	tatuajes (m.)	twenty eight	veininueve
tea	té (m.)	twenty five	veintiseis
teach, show (to)	enseñar	twenty four	veinticinco
teacher	maestra (f.)	twenty one	veintiuno
teacher	maestro/a (m./f.)	twenty seven	veintiocho
teacher's lounge	cuarto de maestras (m.)	twenty six	veintisiete
telephone	teléfono (m.)	twenty three	veinticuatro
television	televisión (f.)	twenty two	veintitres
ten	diez	two	dos
thank you	gracias	two hundred	doscientos
that	ese/a	uncle	tio (m.)
that over there	aquel(la)	under	debajo de
then	entonces	understand	entiende
therapist	terapista (m./f.)	understand (to)	comprender
there	allí	urine	orina (f.)
these	estos/as	use, wear (to)	usar
they	ellos	vaccination	vacunas (f.)
they (f)	ellas	vaccine	vacuna (f.)
thin	delgado/a	vaccine	vacuna (f.)
thirteen	trece	vanilla	vainilla (f.)
thirty	treinta	Vegetables	verduras (f.)

English to Spanish Glossary

verb	verbo *(m.)*
very	muy
violated	violada
violet	violeta
visit *(to)*	visitar
vitamins	vitaminas *(f.)*
vocabulary	vocabulario *(m.)*
vomit *(to)*	vomitar
vowel	vocal *(f.)*
wait *(to)*	esperar
walk *(to)*	caminar
want *(to)*	querer
washcloth	toallita para lavarse *(f.)*
watch, look *(to)*	mirar
water	agua *(m.)*
water	agua *(m.)*
watermelon	sandía *(f.)*
we	nosotros
weak	debil
weak	débil
Wednesday	miércoles *(m.)*
week	semana *(f.)*
what	qué
when	cuándo
where	dónde
which	cuál(es)
white	blanco
who	quién(es)
why	por qué
widowed	viudo/a
wife	esposa *(f.)*
win, earn *(to)*	ganar
wine	vino *(m.)*
with	con
without	sin
woman	mujer *(f.)*
word	palabra *(f.)*
work	trabajo *(m.)*
work *(to)*	trabajar
worker	trabajador *(m.)*
wrist	muñeca *(f.)*
write *(to)*	escribir
written	escrito
year	año *(m.)*
yellow	amarillo
yes	sí
yesterday	ayer
yogurt	yogurt *(m.)*
you (formal)	usted
you (informal)	tú
you all	ustedes
young	joven
you're welcome	de nada
zero	cero

Spanish to English Glossary

a	to, at	arriba de	above
abeja (f.)	bee	artículo (m.)	article
abierto	opened	artístico/a	artistic
abra	open (command)	arvejas (f.)	peas
abril	April	así así	so-so
abrir	open (to)	asistente (m./f.)	para
abuela (f.)	grandmother	asociación (f.)	association
abuelo (m.)	grandfather	aspire	inhale
abuelos (m.)	grandparents	aspirina (f.)	apirin
aburrido/a	bored	asustado/a	frightened
accidente (m.)	accident	atlético/a	athletic
aceite de ricino (m.)	castor oil	auditorio (m.)	auditorium
acuéstese	lay down	ayer	yesterday
adiós	good-bye	ayudar	help (to)
administrador/a (m./f.)	administrator	ayúdeme	help me
agarrar	grab (to)	azúcar (m.)	sugar
agosto	August	azul	blue
agotamiento (m.)	exhaustion	bailar	dance (to)
agua (m.)	water	bajar	lower (to)
agua (m.)	water	baje	lower
agudo	sharp	bajo/a	short
al lado de	beside	baño (m.)	bathroom
alegre	happy	baño (m.)	bathroom
alergia (f.)	allergy	bartitúricos (m.)	barbituates
algo (m.)	something	beber	drink (to)
alguna	some	bebidas (f.)	drinks
allí	there	bendito	blessed
almohada (f.)	pillow	biblioteca (f.)	library
almorzar	have lunch (to)	bibliotecario/a (m./f.)	librarian
almuerzo (m.)	lunch	bien	good
alto/a	tall	billete (m.)	bill
amable	friendly	bistec (m.)	steak
amar	love (to)	blanco	white
amarillo	yellow	boca (f.)	mouth
amigo/a (m./f.)	friend	bombero (m.)	fireman
analgésico (m.)	analgesic	bonito/a	pretty
anaranjado	orange	brazo (m.)	arm
año (m.)	year	brócoli (m.)	broccoli
antes	before	buenas noches	good evening
antiácido (m.)	antacid	buenas tardes	good afternoon
anticonceptivo (m.)	contraceptive	buenos días	good morning
antihemorrágico (m.)	antihemorrhagic	buscar	look for, search (to)
antihistamínico (m.)	antihistamine	búsqueda (f.)	search
antipático/a	mean	cabeza (f.)	head
apio (m.)	celery	caer	fall (to)
aprender	learn (to)	café	brown
aquel(la)	that over there	café (m.)	coffee
aquellos/as	those over there	cafetería (f.)	cafeteria
aquí	here	calabaza (f.)	squash
araña (f.)	spider	calambres (m.)	cramps
árbol genealógico (m.)	family tree	calendario (m.)	calendar
ardiendo	burning	cálmese	calm down

Spanish to English Glossary

calor *(m.)*	hot	cómico/a	funny
cama *(f.)*	bed	comida *(f.)*	food
cambiar	change *(to)*	cómo	how/what
cambio *(m.)*	change	comprar	buy *(to)*
caminar	walk *(to)*	compras *(f.)*	shopping
cansado/a	tired	comprender	understand *(to)*
cantar	sing *(to)*	comprensión *(f.)*	comprehension
cara *(f.)*	face	común	common
carne *(f.)*	meat	con	with
carne de res *(m.)*	beef	con permiso	excuse me
carta *(f.)*	letter	condimentos *(m.)*	condiments
casado/a	married	conductor/a *(m./f.)*	bus driver
catorce	fourteen	congestión *(f.)*	congestion
cebolla *(f.)*	onion	conocer	know (a person/place) *(to)*
cena *(m.)*	dinner	consejero/a *(m./f.)*	counselor
cenar	have dinner *(to)*	consonante *(m.)*	consonant
centavo(s) *(m.)*	cent(s)	constante	constant
cepillo de dientes *(m.)*	toothbrush	contesta *(f.)*	answer
cerca de	near, close to	contestar	answer *(to)*
cerdo *(m.)*	pork	conversación *(f.)*	conversation
cereal *(m.)*	cereal	conversar	converse *(to)*
cerebro *(m.)*	brain	corazón *(m.)*	heart
ceremonia *(f.)*	ceremony	correr	run *(to)*
cereza *(f.)*	cherry	cortar	cut *(to)*
cero	zero	cortesía *(f.)*	courtesy
cerrar	close *(to)*	crampa *(f.)*	cramp
certificado de nacimiento *(m.)*	birth certificate	creer	believe *(to)*
cerveza *(f.)*	beer	crema *(f.)*	cream
chocolate *(m.)*	chocolate	cuál(es)	which
cicatrices *(f.)*	scars	cuándo	when
cien	hundred	cuánto(s)	how much
cierra	close	cuarenta	forty
cinco	five	cuarenta y cinco	fourty five
cinco centavos *(m.)*	nickel	cuarenta y cuatro	fourty four
cincuenta	fifty	cuarenta y dos	fourty two
cincuenta y cinco	fifty five	cuarenta y nueve	fourty nine
cincuenta y cuatro	fifty four	cuarenta y ocho	fourty eight
cincuenta y dos	fifty two	cuarenta y seis	fourty six
cincuenta y nueve	fifty nine	cuarenta y siete	fourty seven
cincuenta y ocho	fifty eight	cuarenta y tres	fourty three
cincuenta y sies	fifty six	cuarenta y uno	fourty one
cincuenta y siete	fifty seven	cuarto *(m.)*	quarter
cincuenta y tres	fifty three	cuarto de maestras *(m.)*	teacher's lounge
cincuenta y uno	fifty one	cuatro	four
cita *(f.)*	appointment	cuatrocientos	four hundred
clase *(f.)*	class	cubierto	covered
cliente *(m/f)*	client	cuello *(m.)*	neck
clínica *(f.)*	clinic	cuesta	cost
cobertor *(m.)*	cover	culebra *(f.)*	snake
cocaína *(f.)*	cocaine	cultura *(f.)*	culture
codeína *(f.)*	codeine	cuñada *(f.)*	sister in law
comer	eat *(to)*	cuñado *(m.)*	brother in law

Spanish to English Glossary

dar	give *(to)*
de	of, from
de nada	you're welcome
debajo de	under
deber	should, owe *(to)*
debil	weak
débil	weak
decidir	decide *(to)*
decir	say, tell *(to)*
dedo *(m.)*	finger
dejar	leave behind *(to)*
delgado/a	thin
dentista *(m./f)*	dentist
dentro de	inside
derecha *(f.)*	right
derecho	straight ahead
desayunar	have breakfast *(to)*
desayuno *(m.)*	breakfast
descanse	rest
descubierto	discovered
desear	desire *(to)*
despacio	slowly
despedida *(f.)*	farewell
despierto	awake
después	after
detrás de	behind
día *(m.)*	day
día festivo *(m.)*	holiday
diálogo *(m.)*	dialogue
diarrea *(f.)*	diarrhea
dicho	said
diciembre	December
diecinueve	nineteen
dieciocho	eighteen
dieciséis	sixteen
diecisiete	seventeen
diente *(m.)*	tooth
diez	ten
diez centavos *(m.)*	dime
dinero *(m.)*	money
dinero en efectivo *(m.)*	cash
dirección *(f.)*	address
director *(m.)*	principal, director
director/a *(m./f.)*	principal
diurético *(f.)*	diuretic
divorciado/a	divorced
doble	bend
doce	twelve
doctor/a *(m./f.)*	doctor
dólar(es) *(m.)*	dollar (s)
dolor *(m.)*	pain
domingo *(m.)*	Sunday
dónde	where
dormir	sleep *(to)*
dos	two
doscientos	two hundred
droga *(f.)*	drug
ducha *(f.)*	shower
duele	hurt
dulces *(m.)*	candy
durazno *(m.)*	peach
edad *(f.)*	age
él	he
ella	she
ellas	they (f)
ellos	they
embarazada	pregnant
emocionado/a	excited
empuje	push
en	in, on
encantar	love (things) *(to)*
encima de	on top of
encontrar	find *(to)*
enero	January
enfermedad *(f.)*	sickness
enfermedad *(f.)*	sickness
enfermera *(f.)*	nurse
enfermero/a *(m./f.)*	nurse
enfermo/a	sick
enfrente de	in front of, facing
enojado/a	angry
enseñar	teach, show *(to)*
entiende	understand
entonces	then
entrar	enter *(to)*
entre	between
entrenador/a *(m./f.)*	coach
erupción *(f.)*	rash
escalofríos *(m.)*	chills
escremento *(m.)*	stool
escribir	write *(to)*
escrito	written
escuchar	listen to *(to)*
escuche	listen
ese/a	that
esos/as	those
espagueti *(m.)*	spaghetti
espalda *(f.)*	back
espárrago *(m.)*	asparagus
espejo *(m.)*	mirror
esperar	wait *(to)*
espire	exhale
esposa *(f.)*	wife
esposo *(m.)*	husband

Spanish to English Glossary

esposos (m.)	spouses	gustar	be pleasing/to like (to)
estado civil (m.)	marital status	hablar	speak (to)
estar	be (to)	hacer	do, make (to)
este/a	this	hamburguesa (f.)	hamburger
estimulante (m.)	stimulant	hecho	done, made
estómago (m.)	stomach	helado (m.)	ice cream
estos/as	these	hermana (f.)	sister
estreñimiento (m.)	constipation	hermanastra (f.)	stepsister
estrugeno (m.)	estrogen	hermanastro (m.)	stepbrother
estudiante (m./f)	student	hermano (m.)	brother
estudiar	study (to)	hermanos (m.)	siblings
expectorante (m.)	expectorant	heroina (f.)	heroin
explicación (f.)	explanation	hielo (m.)	ice
expresar	express (to)	hija (f.)	daughter
expresión (f.)	expression	hijastra (f.)	stepdaughter
extrovertido/a	extroverted	hijastro (m.)	stepson
familia (f.)	family	hijo (m.)	son
famoso/a	famous	hijos (m.)	sons and daughters
farmacia (f.)	pharmacy	hinchado	swollen
febrero	February	hola	hello
fecha (f.)	date	hombre (m.)	man
fiebre (f.)	fever	hora (f.)	hour
fiebre (f.)	fever	hormonas (f.)	hormones
fiesta (f.)	party	hospital (m.)	hospital
forma (f.)	form	hoy	today
formal (m.)	formal	huevos (m.)	eggs
francés (m.)	French	identificación (f.)	identification
frase (f.)	sentence	indicar	indicate (to)
fresas (f.)	strawberries	indigestión (f.)	indigestion
frío (m.)	cold	infectado	infected
frito	fried	inflamado	inflamed
frustrado/a	frustrated	información (f.)	information
fruta (f.)	fruit	informado	informed
fuera de	outside of	informal (m.)	informal
fuerte	strong	inodoro (m.)	toilet
fuerte	strong	insecto (m.)	insect
fumar	smoke (to)	instrucciones (f.)	instructions
galleta (f.)	cookie	inteligente	intelligent
ganar	win, earn (to)	interpretar	interpret (to)
garganta (f.)	throat	introducción (f.)	introduction
gato/a (m./f.)	cat	invitar	invite (to)
gelatina (f.)	jello	izquierda (f.)	left
género (m.)	gender	jabón (m.)	soap
gimnasio (m.)	gymnasium	jale	pull
gordo/a	fat	jamón (m.)	ham
gracias	thank you	joven	young
grande	big	judía verde (f.)	green beans
gris	gray	jueves (m.)	Thursday
gritar	shout (to)	jugar	play (to)
guapo/a	good-looking	jugo (m.)	juice
guardia de seguridad (m./f.)	security guard	julio	July
guardián/a (m./f.)	custodian	junio	June

Spanish to English Glossary

kétchup (m.)	ketchup	mil	thousand
labio (m.)	lip	milla (f.)	mile
laboratorio (m.)	laboratory	millón	million
laboratorio de computadoras (m.)	computer lab	minuto (m.)	minute
lateo (m.)	dairy	mirar	watch, look (to)
laxante (m.)	laxative	mire	look
le	to him, her, you	momento (m.)	moment
leche (f.)	milk	moneda (f.)	coin
leche de magnesia (f.)	milk of magnesia	moneda (f.)	currency
lechuga (f.)	lettuce	morado	purple
leer	read (to)	moreno/a	dark complected
lejos de	far, far from	morfina (f.)	morphine
lengua (f.)	tongue	mostaza (f.)	mustard
levantar	raise (to)	mostrar	show (to)
levante	raise	mucho	much, a lot
levenatese	get up	muela (f.)	molar
llamar	call (to)	muerto	dead
llegar	arrive (to)	muestra	sample
llevar	carry, wear (to)	mueva	move
llover	rain (to)	mujer (f.)	woman
lo	it	muñeca (f.)	wrist
locación (f.)	location	muy	very
luchar	fight (to)	nada	nothing
lunes (m.)	Monday	nadar	swim (to)
madrastra (f.)	stepmother	naranjas (f.)	oranges
madre (f.)	mother	narcótico (m.)	narcotic
maestra (f.)	teacher	nariz (f.)	nose
maestro/a (m./f.)	teacher	náuseas	nauseated
magnesia (f.)	magnesia	negro	black
maíz (m.)	corn	nevar	snow (to)
mal	bad	nieta (f.)	granddaughter
mañana	tomorrow, morning	nieto (m.)	grandson
mano (f.)	hand	nietos (m.)	grandchildren
mantequilla (f.)	butter	ninguna	none
manzanas (f.)	apples	no	no
mareado/a	dizzy	noche (f.)	night
marido (m.)	husband	nosotros	we
martes (m.)	Tuesday	novecientos	nine hundred
marzo	March	noventa	ninety
más	more	noventa y cinco	ninety five
materiales (f.)	materials	noventa y cuatro	ninety four
mayo	May	noventa y dos	ninety two
mayonesa (f.)	mayonnaise	noventa y nueve	ninety nine
media (f.)	half	noventa y ocho	ninety eight
mediano/a	medium	noventa y seis	ninety six
medianoche (f.)	midnight	noventa y siete	ninety seven
medicina (f.)	medicine	noventa y tres	ninety three
mediodía (m.)	noon	noventa y uno	ninety one
melón (m.)	cantaloupe	novia (f.)	girlfriend
menos	less	noviembre	November
mes (m.)	month	novio (m.)	boyfriend
miércoles (m.)	Wednesday	novocaína (f.)	novocain

Spanish to English Glossary

nueve	nine	perro/a (m./f.)	dog
números (m.)	numbers	pescado (m.)	fish
ochenta	eighty	picado	bitten
ochenta y cinco	eighty five	picazón (f.)	itching
ochenta y cuatro	eighty four	pie (m.)	foot
ochenta y dos	eighty two	pierna (f.)	leg
ochenta y nueve	eighty nine	pimienta (f.)	pepper
ochenta y ocho	eighty eight	pintar	paint (to)
ochenta y sies	eighty six	piojo (m.)	lice
ochenta y siete	eighty seven	plátanos (m.)	bananas
ochenta y tres	eighty three	poco	little
ochenta y uno	eighty one	policía (m/f)	police
ocho	eight	pollo (m.)	chicken
ochocientos	eight hundred	poner	put (to)
octubre	October	popote (m.)	straw
oficial (m.)	official	popular	popular
oficina del consejero/a (f.)	counseling office	por favor	please
oficina del enfermero/a (f.)	nurse's office	por qué	why
oído (m.)	inner ear	postres (m.)	desserts
oir	hear (to)	práctica (f.)	practice
ojo (m.)	eye	practicar	practice (to)
olvidar	forget (to)	preferir	prefer (to)
once	eleven	pregunta (f.)	question
operación (f.)	operation	preguntar	ask (to)
oración (f.)	sentence	preparado/a	prepared
oreja (f.)	outer ear	preparar	prepare (to)
orina (f.)	urine	presentación (f.)	introduction, presentation
paciente (m/f)	patient	prima (f.)	cousin (f)
padrastro (m.)	stepfather	primo (m.)	cousin (m)
padre (m.)	father	primos (m.)	cousins
padres (m.)	parents	pronunciación (f.)	pronunciation
palabra (f.)	word	próximo (m.)	next
pan (m.)	bread	psicólogo/a (m./f.)	psychologist
panqueque (m.)	pancake	pulsante	throbbing
papa (f.)	potato	qué	what
parte (f.)	part	quedar	stay (to)
pasar	pass (to)	quemado	burned
pasta (f.)	pasta	querer	want (to)
pastel (m.)	cake	queso (m.)	cheese
pastillas de chupar (f.)	lozenges	quién(es)	who
pastillas para la tos (f.)	cough drops	quince	fifteen
pavo (m.)	turkey	quinientos	five hundred
pedir	request, ask for (to)	radio (f.)	radio
pelirrojo/a	red headed	razón (f.)	reason
pelo (m.)	hair	reacción (f.)	reaction
penicilina (f.)	penicillin	recepción (f.)	reception
pepino (m.)	cucumber	recepcionista (f.)	receptionist
pequeño/a	small	recepcionista (m./f.)	receptionist
peras (f.)	pears	recibir	receive (to)
perder	lose (to)	recomendar	recommend (to)
perdido/a	lost	refresco (m.)	soft drink
perro caliente (m.)	hot dog	regresar	return (to)

Spanish to English Glossary

relájese	relax	sesenta y uno	sixty one
repas (f.)	meals	setecientos	seven hundred
repetir	repeat (to)	setenta	seventy
repite	repeat	setenta y cinco	seventy five
resolver	resolve (to)	setenta y cuatro	seventy four
respire	breathe	setenta y dos	seventy two
respuesta (f.)	answer	setenta y nueve	seventy nine
rojo	red	setenta y ocho	seventy eight
rosado	pink	setenta y seis	seventy six
rosbif (m.)	roast beef	setenta y siete	seventy seven
roto	broken	setenta y tres	seventy three
rubio/a	light complected	setenta y uno	seventy one
sábado (m.)	Saturday	sí	yes
saber	know (a fact) (to)	sientese	sit down
sal (f.)	salt	siete	seven
sal de higuera (f.)	epson salts	sígame	follow me
salchicha (f.)	sausage	sílaba (f.)	syllable
salir	leave (to)	silla (f.)	chair
saliva (f.)	saliva	simpático/a	nice
saludo (m.)	greeting	sin	without
sandía (f.)	watermelon	situación (f.)	situation
sándwich (m.)	sandwich	sobrina (f.)	niece
sangrando	bleeding	sobrino (m.)	nephew
sangrar	bleed (to)	sobrinos (m.)	nieces and nephews
sangre (f.)	blood	soltero/a	single
sano/a	healthy	sonido (m.)	sound
satisfecho	satisfied	suegra (f.)	mother in law
sección (f.)	section	suegro (m.)	father in law
secreción (f.)	secretion	sulfa (f.)	sulfa
sedantes (m.)	sedatives	supositorio (m.)	suppository
seguir	follow (to)	sustantivo (m.)	noun
seguro (m.)	insurance	talentoso/a	talented
seguro de médico (m.)	medical insurance	también	also
seis	six	tapa (f.)	lid
seiscientos	six hundred	tarde (f.)	afternoon, late
semana (f.)	week	tarea (f.)	homework
señor (m.)	Mr., sir	tatuajes (m.)	tattoos
señora (f.)	Mrs., ma'am	taza (f.)	cup
señorita (f.)	Miss	té (m.)	tea
septiembre	September	tele (f.)	tv
ser	be (to)	teléfono (m.)	telephone
serio/a	serious	teléfono celular (m.)	cell phone
serpiente (m.)	snake	televisión (f.)	television
sesenta	sixty	tener	have (to)
sesenta y cinco	sixty five	terapista (m./f.)	therapist
sesenta y cuatro	sixty four	terminar	finish (to)
sesenta y dos	sixty two	tía (f.)	aunt
sesenta y nueve	sixty nine	tímido/a	timid
sesenta y ocho	sixty eight	tío (m.)	uncle
sesenta y seis	sixty six	tíos (m.)	aunts and uncles
sesenta y siete	sixty seven	toalla (f.)	towel
sesenta y tres	sixty three	toallita para lavarse (f.)	washcloth

Spanish to English Glossary

tocar	touch, play (instrument) (to)
tocino (m.)	bacon
tomar	take (to)
tomate (m.)	tomato
tome	take
tonto/a	foolish
toronja (f.)	grapefruit
torta (f.)	cake/sandwich
tos (m.)	cough
tosa	cough (command)
trabajador (m.)	worker
trabajar	work (to)
trabajo (m.)	work
tradición (f.)	tradition
traducción (f.)	translation
traducir	translate (to)
traer	bring (to)
tranquilizante (m.)	tranquilizer
trece	thirteen
treina y tres	thirty three
treina y uno	thirty one
treinta	thirty
treinta y cinco	thirty five
treinta y cuatro	thirty four
treinta y dos	thirty two
treinta y nueve	thirty nine
treinta y ocho	thirty eight
treinta y seis	thirty six
treinta y siete	thirty seven
tres	three
trescientos	three hundred
triste	sad
tú	you (informal)
un centavo (m.)	penny
uña (f.)	fingernail
uno	one
usar	use, wear (to)
usted	you (formal)
ustedes	you all
uvas (f.)	grapes
vacuna (f.)	vaccine
vacuna (f.)	vaccine
vacunas (f.)	vaccination
vainilla (f.)	vanilla
veininueve	twenty eight
veinte	twenty
veinticinco	twenty four
veinticinco centavos (m.)	quarter
veinticuatro	twenty three
veintiocho	twenty seven
veintiseis	twenty five
veintisiete	twenty six
veintitres	twenty two
veintiuno	twenty one
vendedor (m.)	seller
vender	sell (to)
venir	come (to)
ver	see (to)
verbo (m.)	verb
verdad (f.)	truth
verde	green
verduras (f.)	vegetables
viajar	travel (to)
viejo/a	old
viernes (m.)	Friday
vino (m.)	wine
violada	violated
violeta	violet
visitar	visit (to)
visto	seen
vitaminas (f.)	vitamins
viudo/a	widowed
vivir	live (to)
vocabulario (m.)	vocabulary
vocal (f.)	vowel
volar	fly (to)
vomitar	vomit (to)
y	and
yo	I
yodo (m.)	iodine
yogurt (m.)	yogurt
zanahorias (f.)	carrots

La clave de respuestas

Answer Key

"The answer key will help you to know if you have the correct answers for the exercises in the workbook."

La pronunciación - page 10

D. A Escuchar
1. v<u>a</u>c<u>a</u> 2. c<u>e</u>br<u>a</u> 3. b<u>o</u>ls<u>a</u> 4. L<u>i</u>br<u>e</u> 5. arc<u>o</u>í<u>ri</u>s

Formal e informal –page 13

A. Identificación
1. usted 2. tú 3. usted 4. usted 5. tú 6. tú 7. usted 8. usted 9. tú 10. tú

The Wall That Divides Us -page 14

A. La Cultura
1. *Answers may vary.* (Example: Stereotypes, Negative Facial Expressions, etc.)
2. interpersonal communication (facial expression and body language), tone of voice, eye contact
3. eye contact, greet everyone, show respect
4. words do not match interpersonal communication
5. to send positive messages and build trust

Saludos y presentaciones- page 17

A. Saludos
1. Buenos días. 2. Buenas noches. 3. Buenas noches. 4. Buenas tardes. 5. Buenos días.

B. Cortesía
1.mal 2. muy bien 3. así-así 4. muy mal 5. bien

E. Diálogo
Diálogo 1:
Nurse: Good afternoon. My name is Marisa. What is your name?
Patient: My name is Humberto Castillo.
Nurse: Pleased to meet you, Señor Castillo. How are you?
Patient: So-so.
Nurse: Wait a moment, please.

Diálogo 2:
Teacher: Good morning. What is your name?
Student: My name is Juan.
Teacher: My name is Irene. Nice to meet you, Juan.
Teacher: How are you?
Student: Very bad. I have a bad grade.
Teacher: One moment please.

F. Diálogo
Recepcionista: Buenos días. Me llamo Alicia. ¿Cómo se llama?
Cliente: Me llamo Jorge Rodríguez.
Recepcionista: Mucho gusto. ¿Cómo está?
Cliente: No estoy bien. Muy mal.
Recepcionista: Espera un momento por favor.

G. Traducción
Doctor: Good morning.
Patient: Hello.
Doctor: How are you?
Patient: Good, thank you. And you?
Doctor: Very good. What is your name?

H. Reacciones
Answers may vary.
1. Hola 2. Me llamo Juan. 3. Buenas tardes. 4. Hasta pronto. Adiós. 5. Bien, gracias. 6. Buenos días. 7. Mucho gusto. 8. Adiós. 9. Bien, gracias. 10. Hola.

I. ¿Cómo está?
Answers may vary.
1. bien 2. muy mal 3. asi-asi 4. mal 5. muy bien

Expresiones de cortesía- page 25

A. Traducción
1. H 2. E 3. K 4. C 5. I 6. G 7. A 8. J 9. D 10. F 11. B 12. M 13. L

B. ¿Cómo se dice?
1. ¿Cómo se dice...? 2. Lo siento. 3. Sí. 4. Repite, por favor. 5. Gracias. 6. ¿Entiende usted? 7. De nada. 8. ¿Habla inglés? 9. No entiendo. 10. Con permiso.

Pack Your Bags- page 28

A. Palabras Importantes
Answers may vary.
1. No, only 10%-20%. 2. Communicate with the key words 3. Remember key words

Los números- page 30

A. Número de teléfono
1. cinco, siete, tres, tres, nueve, dos, siete
2. cuatro, cinco, tres, nueve, siete, cero, cuatro
3. uno, dos, nueve, seis, siete, cinco, cuatro
4. ocho, tres, seis, cero, cinco, ocho, cuatro
5. dos, seis, nueve, tres, cinco, seis, seis
6. ocho, cero, dos, ocho, cuatro, nueve, cinco

B. Escribir
1. 392-7019 2. 485-1760 3. 593-1860 4. 724-5643 5. 198-0572 6. 463-8095

C. Asociaciones
1. f 2. s 3. j 4. r 5. g 6. h 7. p 8. n 9. m 10. q 11. t 12. e 13. o 14. i 15. a 16. l
17. d
18. b 19. c 20. k

D. Asociaciones
1. f 2. s 3. j 4. r 5. g 6. h 7. p 8. n 9. m 10. q 11. t 12. e 13. o 14. i 15. a 16. l
17. d
18. b 19. c 20. k

E. La clase
1. cuarenta y dos estudiantes 2. veintiocho papeles 3. noventa y uno sillas 4. treinta y siete mesas
5. setenta y cuatro casas 6. cincuenta y nueve plumas 7. ochenta y tres libros 8. sesenta y cinco diccionarios

F. Traducción
1. 253 2. 871 3. 1,526 4. 4,789 5. 3,434,942

161

G. Números
1. setecientos cuarenta y tres 2. doscientos cincuenta y uno 3. mil, trescientos noventa y ocho
4. cinco mil, ochocientos treinta y seis 5. dos millones, novecientos treinta y siete mil,
cuatrocientos diecisiete

H. Matemáticas
1. ciento cincuenta y doscientos son trescientos cincuenta 2. doscientos diez y ciento treinta
son trescientos y cuarenta 3. cuatrocientos y doscientos cuarenta son seiscientos cuarenta 4.
quinientos y quinientos son un mil 5. setecientos y cien son ochocientos 6. mil quinientos y
cinco mil quinientos son siete mil

El Género- page 38

A. Identificaciones
1. feminine 2. feminine 3. masculine 4. masculine 5. masculine 6. masculine 7. feminine
8. masculine

Los artículos- page 40

A. Que es
1. la blusa 2. Las latas 3. El libro 4. El dinero 5. El muchacho 6. El papel 7. Las
computadoras 8. La ropa

B. La clase
1. la 2. Las 3. La 4. Los 5. El 6. La 7. Los 8. Las 9. Los 10. Las 11. El 12. Los 13. Los 14.
La 15. Las 16. La

C. Los Artículos
1. el libro 2. los libros 3. un libro 4. unos libros 5. la mesa 6. las mesas 7. una mesa
8. unas mesas 9. la clase 10. las clases 11. una clase 12. unas clases 13. el carro 14. los
carros
15. un carro 16. unos carros 17. la ventana 18. las ventanas 19. una ventana 20. unas
ventanas

D. Identificación
1. el carro 2. un carro 3. los carros 4. unos carros 5. la pluma 6. una pluma 7. las plumas
8. unas plumas 9. el libro 10. un libro 11. los libros 12. unos libros 13. la mesa 14. una
mesa 15. las mesas
16. unas mesas

La familia- page 44

A. Mi familia
1. tío 2. hermana 3. primo 4. hijo 5. hija 6. abuelo

B. La familia de Ana
1.cierto 2. falso – Monica es la hermana de Ana. 3. falso - Elena es la madre de Ana. 4. cierto
5. Falso - Elena es la madre de Paco. 6. cierto 7. cierto 8. falso - Manuel y Isabel son esposos.
9. cierto 10. falso - Carlos es el hijo de Felipe y Lola.

C. ¿Cómo se llama?
1.Elena 2. Víctor 3. Manuel, Isabel, Felipe, y Lola 4. Francisco y Juanita 5. Celia y Juanita

D. ¿Quién es?
1. Roberto es el hijo de Eduardo y Alicia y el esposo de Gloria. 2. Estela es la hija de Eduardo y Alicia y la esposa de Raúl. 3. Ana es la hermana de Jorge y David y la sobrina de Raúl y Estela. 4. Patricia es la prima de Jorge, Ana, y David y la hija de Roberto y Gloria. 5. David es el nieto de Eduardo y Alicia y el hermano de Jorge y Ana.

E. Estado civil
1. casada 2. soltera 3. soltero 4. casada 5. casado

High vs. Low Emotive Personalities- page 49

A. La comunicación
1. Communication styles are important for communicating effectively.
2. A high emotive person reads body language, are not direct in speaking. They are focused more on non-verbal communication.
3. A low emotive person is more direct and communicates with words more than body language.
4. Answers will vary.
5. Use gestures, look at them, and raise your voice a little.
6. Ask them to explain.

Los días, las meses, y las fechas- page 51

A. Vocabulario
1. semana 2. días 3. meses 4. (answers may vary 5. (answers may vary) 6. (answers may vary)

B. Los días
1. miércoles, viernes 2. domingo, martes 3. viernes, domingo 4. martes, jueves 5. sábado, lunes 6. lunes, miércoles 7. jueves, sábado

C. Los meses
1. jueves 2. diciembre 3. *answers may vary* 4. febrero 5. junio, julio, agosto 6. mayo, domingo
7. lunes

E. Los meses
el invierno- diciembreenerofebrero
la primavera- marzoabrilmayo
el verano- juniojulioagosto
el otoño- septiembreoctubrenoviembre

F. Días y meses
1. domingo 2. lunes 3. Navidad – diciembre Día de los padres – junio Día de gracias - noviembre
Día de San Valentín – febrero Cinco de Mayo – mayo 4. miércoles 5. agosto/septiembre 6. martes

G. La fecha
1. El veintiséis de julio de dos mil trece. 2. El ocho de agosto de mil novecientos ochenta y nueve. 3. El cuatro de marzo de mil novecientos noventa y siete. 4. El catorce de enero de dos mil dos. 5. El veintisiete de mayo de mil novecientos noventa y nueve.

H. Días festivas
1. El catorce de febrero. 2. El veinticinco de diciembre. 3. El primero de enero. 4. El cuatro de julio. 5. El treinta y uno de octubre.

I. Las citas
1. Su cita es el diez de abril de dos mil quince. 2. Su cita es el diecisiete de junio de dos mil catorce.
3. Su cita es el nueve de septiembre de dos mil quince. 4. Su cita es el veintiuno de noviembre de dos mil catorce.

¿Qué hora es? - page 58

A. ¿Qué hora es?
1. Son las tres de la tarde. 2. Son las cinco y cincuenta de la tarde. 3. Son las siete y cuarto de la mañana. 4. Son las ocho de la mañana. 5. Son las seis y media de la noche. 6. Son las diez y diez de la mañana. 7. Son las cuatro y cuarto de la tarde. 8. Es mediodía. 9. Son las siete y cuarenta y cinco de la noche. 10. Es medianoche.

B. ¿Qué hora es?
1. Son las doce y treinta y cinco. 2. Son las diez y diez. 3. Son las ocho y diez.
4. Son las cinco y cincuenta.

C. ¿A qué hora comes?
1. A las once y cinco de la noche. 2. A la una y veinte de la mañana. 3. A las nueve y treinta y cinco de la mañana. 4. A las seis y cuarenta de la noche. 5. A las dos de la mañana. 6. A medianoche.

D. ¿A qué hora?
1. Yo leo el periódico a las cinco y veinticinco de la mañana. 2. Yo abro la escuela a las siete y treinta y cinco de la mañana. 3. Yo estudio el domingo a las seis y cuarenta de la tarde. 4. Mi hija regresa a medianoche. 5. Yo miro la telenovela a la una y veinte de la tarde. 6. El niño bebe la leche a las diez y media de la tarde. 7. Yo como en el trabajo a mediodía. 8. Los estudiantes llegan a la escuela a las ocho y cuarenta y cinco de la mañana.

La escuela- page 62

A. ¿Quién es?
1. la bibiotecaria 2. La maestra 3. El guardián 4. La receptionista 5. El guardia de seguridad 6. La enfermera 7. El director 8. El conductor 9. La maestra 10. El entrenador 11. El asistente

B. ¿Qué cuarto?
1. H 2. A 3. J 4. G 5. D 6. I 7. C 8. B 9. F 10. E

D. A Leer
1. Cursos Básicos
2. Cursos Especializados y Tecnológicos
3. seis
4. electronics, photography, mechanics, carpentry, plastic arts, computation
5. literature, calculous, biology, astronomy, chemistry, geography, fine arts, sociology, psychology, philosophy

F. Identifica
1. bandera 2. pupitre 3. bolígrafo 4. tijeras 5. cuaderno 6. lápiz

G. En la escuela
1. el lápiz 2. la maestro 3. la pluma 4. el diccionario 5. el estudiante 6. el cuaderno 7. la papel
8. el escritorio 9. el pizarra 10. la silla

Palabras interrogativas- page 74

A. Traducción
1. ¿Por qué? 2. ¿Dónde? 3. ¿Cómo? 4. ¿Qué? 5. ¿Cuándo? 6. ¿Quién? 7. ¿Cuál? 8. ¿Cuánto?

B. Situación
1. ¿Qué? ¿Cómo? 2. ¿Por qué? 3. ¿Quién? 4. ¿Cuál? 5. ¿Cuánto? 6. ¿Cómo? 7. ¿Dónde?
8. ¿Cuándo? 9. ¿Cuánto? 10. ¿Dónde? 11. ¿Por qué? 12. ¿Dónde? 13. ¿Cuándo?

Preguntas para la registración- page 78

A. Cierto/Falso
1. falso 2. falso 3. falso 4. falso 5. falso 6. falso

Los Partes del Cuerpo – page 81

A. Los partes del cuerpo
1. finger 2. nose 3. leg 4. arm 5. foot 6. eye 7. hair 8. shoulders 9. head 10. fingernails 11. elbow 12. knee 13. wrist 14. hip 15. mouth 16. outer ear 17. tongue 18. waist 19. toes 20. back

B. ¿Qué parte?
1. cabeza 2. piernas o pies 3. uñas 4. dedos de pie 5. cintura 6. hombros 7. estómago y pecho 8. cuello 9. nalga or cadera 10. espalda

C. Pates interiores
1.la garganta 2. la muñeca 3. la pierna 4. el corazón 5.la columna vertebral 6. el hígado 7. la páncreas
8. el corazón 9. el cerebro 10. el estómago

D. ¿Dónde está?
1. heart 2. lungs 3. kidneys 4. stomach 5. intestines 6. appendix 7. brain 8. throat 9. spleen 10. esophagus 11. gall bladder 12. bone 13. bladder 14. spinal columna

F. ¿Dónde le duele?
1. Me duele el ojo. 2. Me duele el estómago. 3. Me duele el pie. 4. Me duele la pierna.

G. ¡Me duele!
1. Me duele el estómago. 2. Me duele el pie. 3. Me duele la mano. 4. Me duelen los dientes. 5. Me duele la cabeza. 6. Me duele el brazo. 7. Me duele la pierna. 8. Me duele la garganta.

Los Dolores – page 91

A. La traducción
D: My name is Dr. Jones. Do you hurt?
P: Yes, I hurt a lot.
D: Does your arm hurt?
P: No, my arm doesn't hurt.
D: Does your throat hurt?
P: No, my throat doesn't hurt.
D: Does your head hurt?
P: No, my head doesn't hurt.
D: Where do you hurt?
P: My toe hurts.

B. Más dolores
1. ¿Tiene usted dolor de garganta? No, no tengo dolor de garganta.
¿Tiene usted dolor de espalda? No, no tengo dolor de espalda.
¿Tiene usted dolor de cabeza? No, no tengo dolor de cabeza.
¿Tiene usted dolor de ojos? No, no tengo dolor de ojos.
¿Tiene usted dolor de hombros? No, no tengo dolor de hombros.

2. ¿Tiene usted dolor de pierna? No, no tengo dolor de pierna.
¿Tiene usted dolor de pecho? No, no tengo dolor de pecho.
¿Tiene usted dolor de brazo? No, no tengo dolor de brazo.
¿Tiene usted dolor de dedo de pie? No, no tengo dolor de dedo de pie.
¿Tiene usted dolor de cuello? No, no tengo dolor de cuello.

C: Los dolores
1. María le duele la nariz.
2. Fernando le duele la mano.
3. Yo me duele la lengua.
4. Jorge le duele el oído.
5. Usted le duele el pulgar.

D. Identificación
1. pulmones 2. corazón 3. dientes 4. boca, lengua, dientes 5. mano

E. ¿Dónde te duele?
1. ¿Te duele el pulgar? Sí, me duele el pulgar.
2. ¿Te duele la pierna? Sí, me duele la pierna.
3. ¿Te duele el ojo? Sí, me duele el ojo.

Las citas – page 95

A. ¿Cierto o falso?
1. cierto 2. falso 3. falso 4. cierto 5. falso 6. falso

B. Una traducción
Receptionist: Good afternoon.
Patient: Good afternoon. I would like to see the doctor.
Receptionist: Do you have an appointment today?
Patient: Yes, I have an appointment at eleven fifteen.
Receptionist: Good. With which doctor?
Patient: With Dr. Jones.
Receptionist: Fill out this form and sign here, please.
Patient: Thank you. Where is the bathroom?
Receptionist: Follow me, please.
Patient: Thank you.
Receptionist: Did you bring your medical insurance?
Patient: Yes.
Receptionist: The doctor will see you in a minute. Have a seat, please.

C. ¿Cuándo es mi cita?:
1. Su cita es el nueve de mayo del dos mil catorce. 2. Su cita es el primero de julio del dos mil dieciséis. 3. Su cita es el cuatro de octubre del dos mil quince. 4. Su cita es trece de diciembre del dos mil catorce. 5. Su cita es el diecinueve de enero del dos mil dieciséis.

D. ¿Cierto o falso?
1. cierto 2. falso 3. falso 4. cierto 5. cierto

E. ¿Cuál respuesta?
1. D 2. E. 3. B 4. A 5. C

La historia médica – page 100

A. ¿Tiene problemas?
1. ¿Tiene problemas con los ojos? 2. ¿Tiene problemas con los riñones? 3. ¿Tiene problemas con el estómago? 4. ¿Tiene problemas con los orejas/los oídos? 5. ¿Tiene problemas con el corazón? 6. ¿Tiene problemas con los pulmones?

B. ¿Cuáles problemas tiene usted?
1. ¿Tiene problemas con la visión? 2. ¿Toma alcohol? 3. ¿Tiene problemas con la corazón?
4. ¿Tiene problemas con la respiración? 5. ¿Cuándo fue la última vez que recibió la vacuna antitetánica?
6. ¿Has estado hospitalizado alguna vez?

C. ¿Cómo se dice?
1. ¿Toma alcohol? 2. ¿Cuál es su tipo de sangre? 3. ¿Tiene problemas con el corazón? 4. ¿Usa drogas? 5. ¿Tiene alergias? 6. ¿Tiene problemas con la visión? 7. ¿Tiene problemas con la respiración? 8. ¿Fuma usted? 9. ¿Ha estado hospitalizado alguna vez? 10. ¿Tiene problemas con los oídos?

Las síntomas – page 104

A. Las traducciones
1.j 2. l 3. e 4. m 5. h 6. k 7. a 8.o 9. d 10. l 11. c 12.b 13.g 14. q 15.p 16. n 17. f.

B. Más traducciones
1. ¿Tiene un tos? 2. ¿Tiene una fiebre? 3. ¿Estás embarazada? 4. ¿Tiene congestión en los pulmones? 5. ¿Tiene dolor aquí? 6. ¿Tiene dolor en la garganta? 7. ¿El tiene problemas emocionales? 8. ¿Ella tiene dificultad a respirar? 9. ¿El tiene dolor de cabeza? 10. ¿Ella tiene frio?
11. ¿El tiene calor? 12. ¿Está débil?

La enfermedad y la lesión – page 109

A. Un diálogo
E: Good evening. Do you speak Spanish?
P: Good evening. Yes, I speak Spanish.
E: How are you?
P: Very bad.
E: Where do you hurt?
P: I have a head ache.
E: When did the pain start?
P: Yesterday, in the afternoon.
E: Has it happened before?
P: Yes. Two times.
E: Have you thrown up?
P: Yes.
E: Did you have an accident?
P: No.
E: Are you taking medicine?
P: Yes, aspirin.
E: Are you allergic to medication?
P: Yes, penicillin
E: Thank you. The doctor will be with you in a minute.

B. Dos diálogos
R: Good morning. Do you speak English?
P: No.
R: I speak a little Spanish. How can I help you?
P: I would like to see the doctor.
R: Do you have an appointment today?
P: Yes, I have an appointment with the doctor at eleven o'clock.
R: What is your doctor's name?
P: Dr. Smith.
R: What is your name?
P: My name is Rafael Santos.
R: Fill out this form, please.
P: Thank you.
R: Your welcome.
The patient fills out the form.
R: Thank you. Follow me, please.
P: Ok.
R: The doctor will see you in a moment.
The patient waits.
E: Good morning Mr. Santos. My name is Hazel.
P: Nice to meet you.
E: Nice to meet you. How are you?
P: Very bad. I hurt.
E: Where do you hurt?
P: I have a head ache.
E: When did the pain begin?
P: Today in the morning.
E: Has this happened to you before?
P: No.
E: Are you taking any medicines?
P: Yes. I take Tylenol.
E: Are you allergic to any medicines?
P: No.
E: Do you have chest pain?
P: No.
E: Do you have a fever?
P: No.
E: Do you have a cough?
P: No.
E: Ok. The doctor will see you in a minute.
P: Thank you.

Instrucciones para el paciente – page 113

A. Las traducciones
1. urine sample 2. otra vez 3. take off your clothes 4. una muestra de la sangre 5. stool sample 6. respire profundo 7. sit down 8. Cierra 9. to the right 10. tos 11. relax 12. haga como yo 13. open 14. espire 15. to the left 16. levántese 17. lay down

B. ¿Cómo se dice?
1. Q 2. G 3. F 4. N 5. J 6. O 7. K 8. A 9. S 10. L 11. D 12. P 13. E 14. R 15. B 16. I 17. C 18. T 19. M 20. H

El cuarto de hospital – page 118+

A. En el hospital
1. taza 2. almohada 3. toalla 4. cama 5. jabón 6. popote, taza, agua

B. ¿Qué necesito?
1. toallita para lavarse, jabón 2. cepilla de dientes, pasta de dientes 3. televisión 4. cama, cubiertas, almohada 5. silla 6. taza, vaso, agua, popote 7. comida, plato

C. Las instrucciones
1. Acuéstese a la derecha y levantase el brazo. 2. Acuéstese completamente y baje la cabeza.
3. Siéntese y no se mueva. 4. Quitase la ropa y acuéstese a la izquierda. 5. Mueva el brazo y indique dónde le duele.

D. En el cuarto
1. inodoro 2. vaso, agua, popote 3. baño 4. cama, cubiertas, almohada 5. cubiertas 6. cepillo de dientes, pasta de dientes

Made in the USA
Middletown, DE
18 January 2023

22446461R00097